Teach the Recorder:

A Companion to the 'Play the Recorder' Series

Robert Salkeld

Peacock Press

Teach the Recorder: *A Companion to the 'Play the Recorder' Series*
Copyright © 2008 by Robert Salkeld

Acknowledgement
The music examples and the photographic portrait by Mark Gerson are
reprinted with permission from *Play the Recorder*, Books 1 and 2,
by Robert Salkeld, 1966, International Music Publications Ltd., London.
Copyright 2009 and 2012 by Faber Music Ltd.

ISBN 978-1-912271-38-2

Published by Peacock Press, 2019
Scout Bottom Farm
Mytholmroyd
Hebden Bridge HX7 5JS (UK)

Design and artwork by DM Design and Print

PUBLISHER'S NOTE
The music examples labelled "Book 1" and "Book 2" throughout this work refer to the following:
Robert Salkeld, Play the Recorder, Book 1. Faber Music Ltd., revised edition 2009;
Robert Salkeld, Play the Recorder, Book 2. Faber Music Ltd., revised edition 2012.

Teach the Recorder:

A Companion to the 'Play the Recorder' Series

Robert Salkeld

Peacock Press

Dedicated to
John Turner

Illustrations

Portrait of RS. *Mark Gerson Studio, London, 1965.*

RS on the causeway to Lindisfarne, Northumberland during a cycling tour, 1938.

RS and daughter Elizabeth, age 8 years. Laverstock Down, Salisbury, Wiltshire, 1980. *Photo: Bridget, wife of RS.*

RS in the Adjudicator's chair, believed to be at the Suffolk Music Festival, mid-1950s. *Press photo.*

RS at the Gatehouse, Bishopsthorpe Palace, North Yorkshire, during a cycling tour, August 1939.

RS playing a Niendorf piano at the Pinkney residence, Gosforth, Newcastle-upon-Tyne, 1936. *Photo: William Ferrier T. Pinkney, FRPS.*

Tutors, Orff-Schulwerk Course for Teachers, Lady Mabel College, Wentworth Woodhouse, Rotherham, Yorkshire, August 1965. *Left to right:* Robert Salkeld, Marjorie Blackburn (now Marjorie Ayling), Diana Jordan (dance), and Margaret Murray, founder of the Orff Society UK.

Contents

Photo: Mark Gerson

Introduction

Be not afeard; the isle is full of noises,
Sounds and sweet airs, that give delight, and hurt not.[1]

The recorder is a deceptively simple musical instrument. This apparent simplicity has often proved a handicap. Mechanically it is fairly easy to learn; aurally it is no different from other wind instruments.

Because the notes are not fixed they must be 'made', and an intonation awareness and tone sense assiduously acquired. The breath can bring life only if the ear is in control. Educationally this situation presents a rare opportunity and a responsibility; at one and the same time it offers considerable scope for success or failure.

In Schools

A cheap, portable melodic instrument such as the recorder can be a very positive asset, and fruitful work is possible in small, or even quite large groups, when there is informed teaching on good instruments.

Being comparatively easy to learn in the early stages, children who are less able intellectually can learn this instrument than would be advisable in the violin class. All things being equal, such children find enjoyment, and benefit socially.

Personal and group discipline is inherent in the pursuit of a successful combined sound, and young people respond to this. A consciousness of achievement stimulates a desire for further hard work. To gain this sense of growing power, children need opportunities for displaying their prowess before their peers.

Communal occasions offer a special opportunity and incentive, e.g. plays, prize-givings, but none more than the school assembly, where music can be part of the daily life, and a high standard is wished for without thought of applause.

Elementary players can achieve excellent results from a small selection of notes when delivered with clarity and good intonation; while systematic and informed teaching can produce work equal in standard to that of all other musical instruments.

---

1   *The Tempest* III, ii, 146

Point of view

Since its revival the recorder has been the cause of much discomfort. Concern about unmusical playing is not confined to professional musicians; amateurs friendly towards the recorder notice the gulf between it and other instruments. Even devotees feel disappointment that the standard of performance generally is not higher. In some cases a love-hate relationship exists, which is hard to change.

It is known, that compared to other instruments, huge numbers of recorders are bought and played, and that teaching them in schools is encouraged (if not always financed) by most Education Authorities. With so much time and energy expended, the end-product could reasonably be expected to be better. Why 'music and the recorder' are so often incompatible is a puzzle to many; that recorder playing in schools should so often lack competence and refinement is a disappointment to many listeners.

The recorder in school

1. Teachers have been key figures during the re-introduction of the recorder, yet they themselves have expressed doubts about standards, and their fitness to teach the new instrument. The present difficulties are not of the teachers' own making: had the recorder been better taught at the outset, the situation would be different.

2. Because of the 19th-century gap in live teaching, a teacher-pupil tradition did not exist as a pedagogic starting point. However, teaching a class of thirty is quite different from taking an individual pupil.
   Present-day teachers have been further handicapped by the dearth of high standard public performances. And their educational task gained limited help from attending massed meetings of amateur players in London and elsewhere.

3. Today's recorder teachers are only open to criticism if, knowing all is not well, they do nothing to bring class method more into line with other subjects.

4. A syllabus or long-term policy is rarely presented to a new recorder teacher. The assumption is either it is not necessary, or that the teacher knows already. An unspoken understanding exists that a presentable product will be out in public as soon as possible, leaving the hapless teacher immersed in an activity more diffuse in its aims than any other subject on the curriculum.

Moreover, the teacher may wonder why, despite lip-service in praise of music, recorders are often taught (sometimes on the timetable, sometimes off), in rushed dinner-hours, in cloakrooms or after school.

Amateur status

A glance back helps us to understand the present. A number of fortuitous circumstances prevented the recorder getting away to a good start educationally.

(1) Early recorder playing was recreational, technique being of secondary importance; added to which there was a lack of teaching music, and cheap mass-produced plastic instruments had not long been introduced into schools.
   After the disruption of the Second World War, the recorder began its long climb to acceptance as a contemporary instrument. By 1937 enough individual teaching had not been done outside schools for the work to have been spread so freely inside. The information and experience available before and after the War was not enough to sustain widespread, rapid growth. With hindsight this point appears crucial.
   True, some Yorkshire school children had broadcast and performed to the troops, but this and other commendable examples were isolated, and could not have given school teaching in general the impetus and example needed at the time.

(2) With the serious study of recorders excluded from all Music Colleges but one, the increasingly popular instrument found itself curiously poised with one foot in school, and the other in amateur music-making.

Teachers who 'tootled' for pleasure could all too easily switch from an adult gathering to a school recorder group without making a distinction or noticing the difference. Some aspects of the cross-fertilization have been beneficial, but one in particular was detrimental; the mood of superficiality which pervaded the groups, in the belief that 'enjoyment for enjoyment's sake' was a valid basis for instrumental study.

(3)   Frequently the same music was played in school, as out. The young players were accepting an adult taste in composers, and having their technical capabilities measured by an adult, amateur yardstick. The best young players already had the capacity to develop beyond limits set by many teachers. This was especially noticeable in the 1950s, and still applies today.

The instruments

A decisive influence on recorder work during the 'renaissance' was commerce. Recorder playing would not have spread without the business enterprise and persistence of the pioneers, but it was a misfortune that so many inferior instruments (mostly descant) were put into the hands of so many defenceless young people. By a stroke of fate, cheapness rather than quality became the deciding factor in manufacture and marketing.

Being less restricted over choice, today's purchaser is more fortunate. In spite of increased research, and the better quality of mass-produced recorders, the chances of buying a poor (even bad) instrument is still too high. A very large collection of inferior "educational" instruments exists to prove the point; many currently on the market.

What must performances have sounded like on these instruments? What must recorder teaching have been like to have accepted and used recorders as badly out of tune and tone?

Standards

1.   Poor results soon lend to loss of respect. After gaining a significant status in musical history, the recorder is now down-graded. At its lowest level, the instrument favoured by Purcell, Bach, Handel and Telemann has been treated not as a serious musical instrument, but as an educational tool, a stepping stone to something better (usually orchestral woodwind).

2.   Many schools have handled the recorder in bulk, both in ordering and in size of classes — 20–30 for teaching together, and 50–60 in the school hall for occasional events. At adult meetings 100 or more players is nothing unusual. An attitude was established which ignored the step-wise progress accepted as essential for the learning of other instruments.

3.   The recreational stigma led to wrong evaluations of teaching-time in relation to the numbers being taught. An individual piano or violin lesson usually lasts thirty minutes; an over-worked recorder teacher would be lucky to get forty minutes (often less) for a class of thirty ungraded pupils, with no time allowed for arriving and settling, handing out copies, and arranging music-stands.

School work

(1)   The sales talk about the recorder not only being the cheapest instrument available for educational use, but also the easiest, has been a pernicious influence.

As the recorder is so easy,[2] it was unimportant whether a teacher learnt to play before starting to teach. The joke about keeping one lesson ahead was too often true with recorders, and when no one else was available, a class would continue to be taught in this way.

(2)   Recorder teaching in schools being predominately in the hands of non-specialists, even non-players, it is not surprising that less attention was given to sound than to finger charts, rudiments, notation; the recorder often being exploited solely as preparation for life in an orchestra.

The value of teaching the recorder as a musical instrument is lost if the approach is too clinical.

---

2 . 'T'is as easy as lying.' *Hamlet* III, ii, 379.

(3)   There are always notable exceptions, but too often the attitude to class teaching has not been commensurate with the demands and complexities of the task; the main credential having been a spirit of adventure, and an ability to control children. Inevitably, playing standards have suffered.

The common complaint

That the recorder should have caused criticism is not so surprising. Remarks have been made by professional musicians (sometimes in public) and many keen young players have been asked why they do not move on to a 'proper' instrument.

Much of the criticism is prejudiced and ill-informed; but not all. It is exasperating for a teacher who *is* producing good musical playing to hear the remark: "I have nothing against recorders, except that they always play out of tune." Not 'always'; but more often than they ought.

Teaching

Every teacher of a beginners' class has a free choice of direction; in a nutshell, between 'fingers alone' or 'fingers and sound.' Circumstances at school may tempt one to advance too quickly, but when ambition takes over musical playing suffers.

Pupils who are merely digit-happy are missing a great deal.

Conclusion

Recorder playing at festivals and concerts suggests that the past is still with us, and that unless a higher standard is reached more often, the recorder will continue as Cinderella, and the critics will remain unconvinced.

2

Fingering

A. The approach

A beginner is immediately absorbed in the task of covering and uncovering holes. Facing tunes to play, the matter is urgent. Breathing and tonguing are not visible, and are considered to be less important; knowing about these can safely be left till later, or so it would seem.

The bias is understandable but unfortunate. Unless a knowledge of fingering is balanced by an equal concern for sound, a recorder player is not equipped to make music of the same quality as that achieved on other instruments. Teachers can, unintentionally, encourage a finger-chart fixation in their pupils, and by so doing foster an unbalanced view of recorder playing.

Correct coverage of the holes has limited value if breath and tongue do not co-operate, because they control the tonal flow. For there to be real progress, the aural side must be linked to the physical. To play the 'right note' but the wrong sound is a deception which gives the recorder a bad name.

B. Finger movement

1. Finger movement <u>without</u> sound enables the mind to concentrate on the physical; first on table-top, then with recorder resting on chin.

2. Making two adjacent fingers act together is not a simple task when first undertaken. In B–G, imagine LH.3. has to arrive before LH.2. In E–C, curve the hand round slightly.

Book 1*, p.6, no.8

Book 1, p.25, no.14

3. In C¹–D¹ if LH. thumb action is not quick a *portamento* is heard.

Book 1, p.12, no.2

4. If bottom C is difficult to reach, put on RH.4. ahead of the other fingers, e.g., in octaves and wide leaps.

Allegro

Book 2, p.22, no.12

*See Publisher's Note.

5.   Learning a fingering in isolation is not always best; it can be easier to remember a small group of notes. By practising them together, a relationship is established which assists mind and muscle.

6.   When learning some fingerings, especially those which are 'forked', one method is to place on all fingers and then withdraw those not required.

7.   A basic LH movement occurs when ♩ is played. When included in a LH plus RH fingering the 'pincer' movement seldom causes difficulty, e.g., D^1–E^1, D^1–F^1, and D^1–F#^{1}, whereas D^1–G^1 played alone, often does. Because of a need for precision of action, the interval is easier to play detached than legato.

8.   Quick groups of notes combine to form united movements. Some ornaments are assimilated in this way.

Book 2, p.12, no.7.

9.   To develop a technique that endures, finger movements should be repeated till muscular reflexes work without conscious effort.

10. A device which can assist a proficient solo player is the muscular accent; a slight pressure added to the note before a move eases the move itself. The finger acts with a spring-like action the instant the pressure is released.

In an unslurred sequence the performance of repeated patterns can be helped in this way. There must be perfect co-ordination from the tongue.

11. For the teacher, the word 'technique' means: discovering the most appropriate actions for successful playing, and establishing these by purposeful repetition.

C. Muscles

1. Because the physical demand of the recorder is low, little thought is given to muscles. It pays not to under estimate this aspect of playing. Survival is possible for a time, but not indefinitely. Progressing to music requiring greater speed and agility, the playing begins to slow up; the fingers seem to 'get in the way.'

2. In quick music, finger pressure is a real handicap. Even advanced players tend to thrust downwards when the mood is animated.

"The quicker the tempo the more tranquil the fingers" is a useful maxim.

3. On transferring to the recorder, piano and string players press their fingers through force of habit. Neurotic recorder players are unable to relax themselves or their fingers at *any* time!

4. The fingers need only seal the holes. Pressing on the keys after the sound has been produced is known to pianists as 'key-bedding'. Similarly, 'hole-pressing' occurs among recorder players.

5. A player who is musically insecure or nervous will grip, or splay the fingers. Muscular tension can result in making the fingers ache.

6. Keyed-up to grapple with the new experience, beginners can find it hard to relax. Intermediate players can do the same. In fact, all players sometimes stiffen their muscles or bodies at wrong moments.

7. To all but the most experienced, the visual impact of black print (e.g., clusters of quavers) can trigger anxiety, which in turn causes muscles to stiffen. Whilst solo players are most affected, it can happen in class.

    There will be bars or phrases that the majority find difficult, and it saves time if these are isolated for attention before the piece is played through.

8. One of the aims of instrumental teaching is to prevent over-work. The principle is the same for all: 'The maximum result from the minimum of effort'.

9. In quick playing, finger pressure is a real handicap. To demonstrate: play 'For He's a Jolly Good Fellow', as fast as possible, while gripping. Then 'switch off' the fingers, allowing them to move without conscious effort.

Book 1, p.29, no.11.

10. The ability to relax being so necessary, it is surprising to see printed reference to: "downward pressure of the fingers"; fingers "hitting the holes"; "covering the holes tightly"; fingers "coming down like hammers"; even to using fingers "violently". Such advice can only mislead the unwary, especially those who teach themselves.

D. Thumbs

(1)   The idea that both thumbs support the recorder to an equal degree is a source of trouble. The right thumb supports, the left needed for 'pinching', should remain relaxed.

(2)   Some tenor recorders are bigger than others: trebles differ in size, and so do descants. Neither fingers nor thumbs are free when a recorder is too large for a player.

School players who learn treble or tenor before their hands are fully-grown do not achieve a satisfactory working posture. With fingers and thumbs of both hands grasping the instrument, they can feel (and often look) uncomfortable.

(3)   Most adults who 'squeeze', have flat protruding thumbs: the two faults go together. When thumbs are wrongly placed, the hands are less free, and this leads to stiffness. Hands differ in size, but that is not the issue.

(4)   If elbows are winged out from the body, thumbs become horizontal and **less** flexible at the joints. A teacher should look out for this; also for arched wrists.

(5)   The position of both thumbs is important. Many self-taught players have difficulty 'pinching'; nearly always their left thumbs are fixed in impracticable positions. With this altered they soon play 'pinched' notes accurately. (Physically, all thumbs are not the same.)

E. Pinched notes

(a)   Pinch is not the ideal word; better to think of the thumb hole (or octaving hole) as being 'unstopped' (uncovered) rather than 'pinched'.

(b)   Hold the recorder in the right hand, a short distance from the mouth, and crank the left thumb a few times. Notice how easy the action is when the thumb is free.

(c)   The left thumb-nail should be cut rather short. A claw-like nail is not efficient.

(d)   An alternative to the thumb-nail is to slide the pad of the thumb across the hole to allow a crack of air through. Some players prefer this method and use no other. However, the pinching method is the most practical for class teaching. The aperture should be as small a possible.

(e)   Some of the concern over pinching is imaginary. There is no reason why G–G^1 should be more awkward than E–E^1, since G is part of the E fingering. The position on the stave makes G^1 look more difficult!

(f)   Little-finger action only may be needed for a wide interval. Unless a player knows in advance how little work is involved, there may be unnecessary hand movement.
In the following, although the interval is wide, finger movement is small.

● 123/12   ∅ 123/   ● 12/12   ∅ 12/12   ∅ 123/13   ∅ 13/13

(g)   When E¹–A is slurred, left-hand movement must be particularly neat and precise.

Book 2, p.26, no.11.

(h)   As a rule, more interest is shown in fingers, than in thumbs. Thumbs should be kept under observation in class, lest they move too far under the recorder.

(i)   For advanced players, a subtle use of the left thumb operates the intonational control of pinched notes. By widening the aperture notes can be raised in pitch.

Pitch can also be manipulated by fingers: a slight easing off a hole will sharpen; and to flatten, spare fingers can hover above open holes (known as 'shadowing').

F. Alternative fingerings

At one time a curious prejudice against learning alternatives prevented some players acquiring a smooth technique. As a way out it was suggested that 'alternative' meant optional.

Why alternative fingerings are used: —

i)   To facilitate finger movements, and to clarify finger gymnastics in rapid passages, i.e., to make repeated patterns more practical, in quick runs, arpeggios, chromatic scales, and broken chords.

ii)   To eliminate 'clicks' in slurs.

iii)   To aid legato, especially in slurs.

iv)   To alter tone colour.

v)   To vary dynamics.

vi)   To alter the pitch of an imperfectly tuned note.

N.B. A changed fingering produces a note of slightly different pitch to the basic coverage.

A pedantic use of alternatives is no advantage. On the other hand, to play imperfectly for even a short time, is no foundation for future music-making. As important as knowing how to play alternatives, is knowing *when* to play them.

G. Which alternatives?

Should elementary players be introduced to Alternatives? Yes, whenever possible. In class only a few need be in everyday use. On the descant, the primaries are BII (• 2 3) and E¹II (0 0 23 12), and later C¹#II (0 23 12) and BbII (• 13 / 13).

Book.1. p.34, no.5.

Book.1. p.35, no.6.

Book.2. p.4, no.3.

Book.2. p.4, no.2.

Book.1. p.31, no.12.

Book.1. p.32, no.11.

BII removes a 'click' from some slurs, and is willingly accepted for the B–C¹ trill. Those who adopt E¹II can cross 'the break' smoothly, i.e., from unpinched register to the pinched.

To perform the standard repertoire artistically, a solo player needs to be equipped with a choice of fingering to suit specific circumstances. It is not uncommon to meet a student frustrated by lack of previous acquaintance with alternative fingerings.

H. Teaching Drills

1.   Fingering directions can be called using numbers or letters, whichever is applicable at the time.

3   3   6   3   3   6

E   D   C

2.   A direct reference to muscular movement can be vocalised.

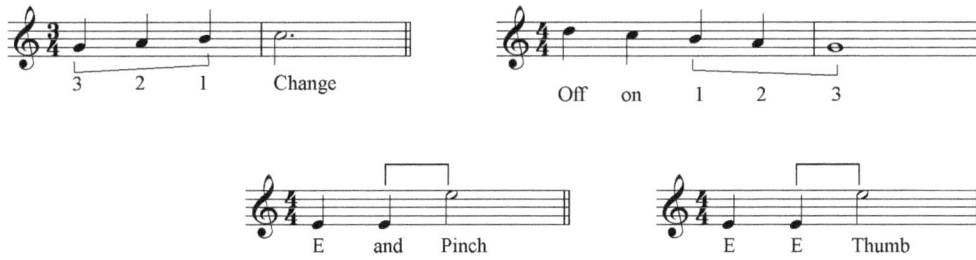

3 2 1   Change   Off   on   1   2   3

E   and   Pinch   E   E   Thumb

I. Conclusion

An elementary player has much to contend with: an unfamiliar object to hold, strange notation, fingerings which interlock, and the strange experience of a flood of sound from other recorders.

It is possible for a teacher to be deceived by the apparent fluency of a class. The members, relying on each other to carry the music through, can give a favourable impression which conceals personal uncertainties.

In a recorder class the 'manipulative-plus-mental' aspect of the task must be carefully nurtured, or a beginner may lose heart, and give up. If recorders were taught like a singing class, the members would be unable to acquire the mental images which lie behind all instrumental playing.

Tonguing

Introduction

The start looks easy. Take a deep breath, and, if there is no slur, 'say' 'T' on each note. The eager pupil remembers this and dutifully 'Tees' the rows of crotchets; after which what happens in the mouth can cease to be of interest.

We all breathe, and our tongue seems to know what to do without being helped; so when learning the recorder these functions appear to be automatic. But the tongue's influence on rhythm and tone-production is crucial, and cannot be ignored. Real music will not emerge without the tongue's contribution, however agile the fingers.

Normal tonguing

1. On a descant recorder the 'T' action is about 1¾ inches behind the starting point of the sound. The instrument maker decides at what angle the breath is 'cut' by the recorder lip,[3] but leaves wind pressure and emphasis to the player.

Any additional disturbance from the tongue can only upset prepared calculations and spoil sound production. Therefore, unless the explosive content of 'T' is reduced to inaudibility, tone will be marred by extraneous sound.

2. A row of four crotchets (all separate and wooden-looking in print) can best be taught first as a semibreve pulsated four times; the 'T' being a tongue movement, not a syllable of speech. Better to convey the idea of fluidity and ease, than to dwell on the attacking action of the tongue. Continuity, not detachment, is the message.

3. For variety, 'T' can be replaced by other tongue movements: 'Do' for gentle, low notes, feminine endings, and legato; 'Too' and 'Loo' can also be used. For upward octaves 'Do–Te' can be adopted as the norm.

Te - Do   Do - Te - Do

Legato tonguing (Mezzo tonguing)

It might be thought that since breath flows directly into the mouthpiece, a song-like *cantabile* is easy to produce, but this is not so. Every performer, without exception, has to work to achieve on the recorder as good a musical line as a singer.

Ignore the tongue and it will not only do too much, it will, in an emergency, forget its responsibility to the breath, and rush to the aid of the fingers. In other words, the tongue, regardless of musical effect, will stop the flow and provide a convenient gap for a player having difficulties with fingering.

a) Slurred legato is created with the tongue in 'Oo' position, but in 'tongued legato' a silent tongue movement is employed on every note. Each sound runs into the next, no gaps allowed. Not slurring, but sounding almost the same as slurs.

Legato tonguing is exacting: it requires complete synchronization of tongue and fingers. For perfect smoothness the tongue movement should be rapid, yet gentle, with the tongue hardly touching the palate.

b) To counter poor legato, a teacher can ask for some playing to be tongue-**less**, if for no other reason than to accustom pupils to the standard of tonal flow expected. Lazy finger movements will be revealed, but this is an advantage. It is noticeable that playing with no tonguing shows up fewer 'clicks' than is expected.

---

3. Labium.

In the exercises, keep the time strict, the tone fluid. Sing to 'ah', then play using the syllable 'Too'. It takes concentration to keep the slurred version as secure in rhythm as the tongued.

Book 1, p.23, no.29.

Book 1, p.31, no.12.

(1) Sing (to "Ah")
(2) Play slurred
(3) Play tongued legato

c)   Legato playing, breathing and phrasing can all be improved by using simple tunes from a songbook or hymnbook. A feeling for vocal shape has great value.

Staccato tonguing

(1)   All notes are ended and started by the tongue. To sing or to dance; that is the question. If to dance, then legato is punctuated by 'stopped' notes (staccato), some of which will be given slight impetus from the tongue. The 'stopped' tonguing syllable 'Tu' (as in Tug) is commonly employed.

(2)   A bad recorder staccato makes a spitting sound; on a bowed instrument a mere grunt or scratch. The true staccato is a chip of tone encased in silence.

T   Tu   T   Tu   T   and   Tu   T____

(3)   The tongue is held an instant on the hard palate, before dropping; obstructing the breath, then releasing it suddenly. Over-action must be avoided. Recorder-playing oboists are inclined to attack the mouthpiece by bringing the tongue forward.

(4)   Three important points, quickly said and easily forgotten:

   (a) All staccato notes are part of their surroundings. Light or firm, they belong to rhythm, and are part of a phrase.

   (b) As silence itself is a form of emphasis, additional emphasis from the tongue may not be required.

   (c) Staccato notes, other than those necessary for interpretation, should not be indulged in.

(5)   The tongue can act percussively; like a finger-tip on a tambourine. There is no harm in knowing this, provided every short note is not given extra emphasis.

In lively dances the tongue tips the palate gently. Tonguing patterns emerge from dance rhythms, and these can usefully be played in advance, on one note.

Book 2, p.22, no.11

(6) An accomplished player will vary the length and strength of staccato; some light, or emphatic, some *staccatissimo* — the choice depending on context.

(7) For clarity, and to save being 'tongue-tied' when playing quick quavers, a solo player can employ double-tonguing: not difficult if practised first on a single note.

In simple language, the syllables are:—

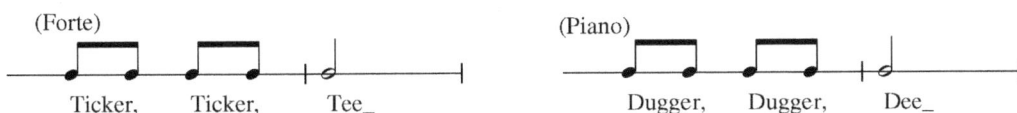

Audible tonguing

1.   In school, playing and learning to read music go hand in hand. The concern over print can cause recorder playing to suffer, with over-confident tonguing going unnoticed. Sad to say, firmness of delivery is not a virtue; it is called 'over-tonguing'.

2.   In large rooms and halls the natural tendency is for players to over-blow. In addition, a loud piano in a large setting is a perfect cloak for strong tonguing.

3.   The over use of the explosive 'T' can become a habit; those with a weak rhythmic sense being likely to seek refuge in mechanical tonguing.

Finding a remedy

1.   There is hope once a hard tonguer has realised that the tongue does not intercept breath and fingers, but helps them to unite. In true legato the tongue binds, it does not separate. Heavy tonguing is not easy to alter, once it has set in.

2.   Unless the tongue can be cured of over-activity it cannot be used purposefully when emphasis is required. — Suggestion: play some phrases without moving the tongue; just pour in breath, concentrating on flow, and ignoring any imperfections. When the ear has accepted the continuity and absence of stress, set the tongue in motion, gently stroking the air-stream as it passes through the mouth. There should be no tension or pressure on the palate, that is the important thing.

3.   'Intoning' can be tried, moving pitch a tone or semitone above or below a single note. As a group exercise it can be supported by discreet chords from the piano. The effect is similar to Plainsong.

4.   Tension in the tongue is eased when 'Do' is adopted in place of 'T'; a gentle action which influences the breath-flow without stopping it.

Rests and note-ends

1. In music, silence is emphatic and can speak as strongly as sound. The tongue, being in control, cuts the air-supply at a rest, a breath mark, and after the final note. The quick, light return to the palate gives the sound its clean tonal-edge. Were the tongue to give music no more, it would still be making an invaluable contribution.

2. An immediate gain in clarity and impact is apparent when an ensemble is unanimous about note-ends. To achieve musical discipline, no sound should ever end untidily. Separate notes, phrase-ends, and in class, even a combined tuning 'A' should end on a time-spot.

3. A clean ending is more difficult to achieve than a clean attack. As note-ends can over-run into rests, precision of tonguing is vital, especially in group-playing.

   For a silence to be felt, every tongue must move at the same time. The pipes instantly obey when an organist lifts his or her hands: a row of recorder players' tongues has the same effect.

Joins in the music

1. These need care, the tongue allowing just enough time for a breath intake, without a slackening of pace or dropping of pitch.

Book 2, p.17, no.4

Book 2, p.19, no.24

either.......

or.......

2. Players with only single stave copies will be unaware of potential untidy spots like the following.*
   Unless an adjustment is made, overlaps at phrase ends will be untidy.

Book 1, p.23, no.28

Teaching points

1. A player with a weak sense of pulse will unconsciously seek refuge in exaggerated tonguing, the firm action giving an illusion of security.

2. The tongue acts as a brake on speed: in class, tempo rarely remains constant when all tonguing is removed. Its absence reveals the strength or weakness of a group's pulse-sense. Re-introduce the tongue, and its effect on tone and delivery is immediately apparent.

3. Over-tonguing is most audible when break pressure is eased. Both tongue and breath must adjust when low notes are played. Over-tonguing combined with over-blowing produces a rough, ungainly sound characteristic of the recorder at its worst. Most musicians would run a mile to escape this.

4. Reminder: some slurred intervals (often upward leaps) produce a 'click', however smoothly fingered. A gentle movement from the tongue remedies this.

5. A roomful of tongues will not synchronize unless clear procedures are adopted, especially when ending held notes. Combined action cannot be left to chance.

A call of "up" or "down-up" can help many tongues unite in action.

6. Combined practice of a single staccato note, using 'Tu', should immediately brighten the sound. Inject tone with the breath, and vary the length of the notes. A row of staccatos can 'bounce' like a ball off the ground.

7. As a visual aid, hand-conducting is valuable. Musical discipline gains when a performance is directed, controlled and shaped from a central point.

The following signals for release are in use:—

a) A small, knife-like gesture of the hand, i.e., a downward movement with straight fingers, which suggests the 'cutting' of sound.

b) A pincer action of fingers and thumb, which indicates the nipping off of sound.

27

c)   Thumb-flicking. A peremptory click can be useful at times.

d)   When playing the recorder: a nod combined with an upward jerk of the instrument.

e)   Hand-raising from the piano keys, etc.

Marking copies

Musical standard benefits from uniformity of editing. Teachers who accept the drudgery, and mark all copies, will be amply rewarded. Players of all grades must be unanimous over articulation, breathing and phrasing. Playing from 'blank' copies (i.e. music which is unedited) is self-defeating, and leads to disappointment.

Decisions are based on style, mood, pulse, rhythm, and fingering demands. In the example from Purcell's *Boree* below: (1) is too suave; (2) though better, is not rhythmic enough; and (3) is best.

(1)

Book 2, p.13, no.13

(2)

(3)

Drum   etc.

Conclusion

The constant accenting of notes by the tongue precludes the musical use of emphasis. Printed recorder music has few markings; much is left to the education and experience of the player, whose responsibility it is to vary tonguings, and so make refined interpretations possible.

Tonguing which is doing no harm, may be doing no good either.

4

Articulation

Introduction

The spacing of notes comes next in importance to the notes themselves. Personal taste and feeling for style influences the frequency of staccatos and the distance between notes. With a group, once decisions have been made and the copies marked, it is essential that the directions be adhered to.

Some solo tunes allow articulation to be varied. 'My Dancing Day' sounds quite well played legato; more effective with a few staccatos added; and best, with well-marked staccatos and accompanied by a small drum.

Detached notes

So far, any note separated from its neighbours has been termed 'staccato'; in fact, every separated note does not require staccato tonguing, it is merely detached.

A string player accepts that some notes are to be played *détaché*; others staccato. The recorder player must also distinguish between the various types of short note.

Repeated notes

1. Repeated notes are of special interest, even in moderate tempi. Light, detached notes are appropriate in lively music, see ex. (1).
2. In group playing, tongues can be lazy on repeated notes. 'Merrily we roll along' is good for inciting a bravura staccato. The rhythm does the teaching. When speed is increased, repeated notes bounce of their own accord, see ex. (2).

3. A class of descants playing in unison can produce pellet-like staccatos, when light, short notes are required. Speech rhythms may be used profitably to illustrate musical emphasis.

Book 1, p.13, no.8.

Octaves

Octaves are similar to repeated notes, and when not slurred need to be handled with precision.

The anacrusis

A staccato up-beat gives rhythm a 'lift-off'. The character of the music will suggest when this is applicable.

(legato)   Book.2, p.5, no.5   Book.2, p.10, no.17

Sometimes the choice is less obvious. Although tunes (2) and (3) need not be staccato, a player with a strong rhythmic sense would feel it appropriate. The choice need not remain the same on each repeat. Soloists use their discretion, but in class, staccato dots should be interpreted according to a pre-arranged plan.

Book. 2, p,10, no.14

Book. 1, p,22, no.26

Duple time

Light, detached notes are advisable in 2/2 time, when the tempo is moderately fast. Lightening the second half of the bar avoids stodginess, and prevents a dance sounding like a march.

Con brio

1.

Book.2, p.25, no.8

Moderately quick

2.

Book.1, p.11, no.9

In (3) a heavy staccato is out of place. Uniform tonguing would weigh the rhythm down and alter the character.

Vivace

3.

Book.2, p.13, no.13

Waltzes and 6/8 time

Separated notes and silences are important in Waltzes, whether by Johann Strauss, or not. Dotted notes are traditional in all quick dance rhythms, especially Gigues.

1.

Book.2, p.19, no.24

Con brio

2.

Book.2, p.22, no.11

Syncopation

Dots are often used in syncopated patterns, sometimes with an emphasis added.

1.

2.

Book.1, p.21, no.21

Common faults

1.   Left without guidance a group will be lazy about staccatos, and regardless of style, 'glue-up' the sound.
2.   Slurs are misinterpreted, when they are read, not as tonguing marks, but as indications of phrasing. N.B. The second of two quavers should only be "chipped" when the style demands.

3.   In (2), with the four-bar phrase in mind, the quavers would be played smoothly and unaccented.

Book.1, p.35, no.8

4.   If encouraged to play quickly too soon, nearly every note can become short. Such playing is not satisfying to listen to. Even in so boisterous a tune as 'For He's a Jolly Good Fellow' it is not effective to rob the crotchets of duration and tone.

Book.1, p.29, no.11

5.   Teachers of class singing will know how unmusical a song sounds when every syllable is accented. Elementary violinists can spoil their sound by accenting each bow change. Likewise, recorder players damage both pulse and shape when they perform 'syllabically'. The stressing of 'Hot Cross Buns' illustrates this:

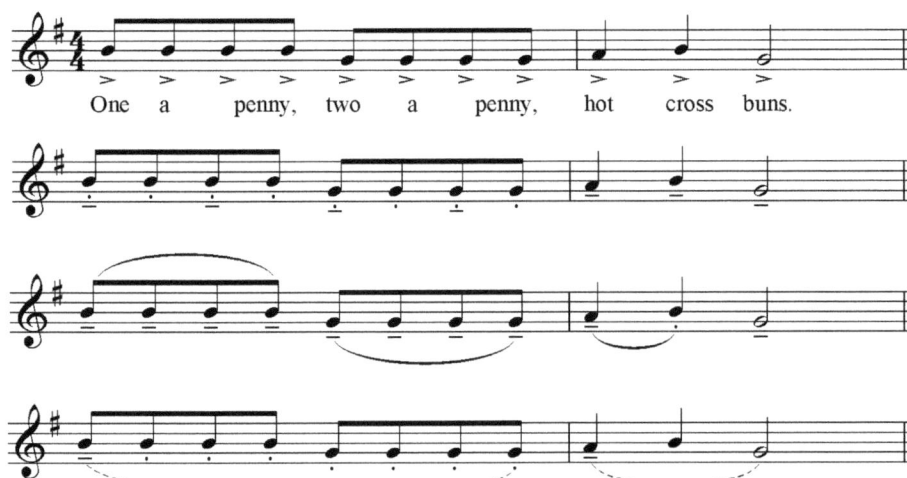

One   a   penny,   two   a   penny,   hot   cross   buns.

[(4) *Over-tongued*

(5) *Stilted*

(6) *Better*

(7) *The best, if tempo quick*]

6.   In solo patterns, one way to be less metrical is to remove emphasis from the first beat of the bar.

Conclusion

1.   A pianist is helped by having phrasing marked by long curved lines. Recorder players are left to work out phrase lengths for themselves, and frequently must add their own articulation.
2.   The recorder is by its nature limited in dynamic range. A player is obliged to rely on musicianship, and should remember that accents are made by breath and tongue, and occasionally by breath alone.
This leaning of the breath on a chosen note may be on a metric beat, but is usually more valuable rhythmically when placed on an off-beat.
3.   'Phrasing is what you say; articulation the way you say it.'— usually there is only one way to phrase, but several different ways to articulate.

5

Breathing

Introduction

It is said that whereas fingers can be trained, and tongues disciplined, the breath must be educated. The balance is a fine one, both in playing and teaching.

Some have good tone and spoil it by over-tonguing, others have agile fingers but poor breath control.

————————————

About the recorder, Shakespeare's Hamlet said: "Give it breath with your mouth, and it will discourse most eloquent music."[4] To prove him right, two points should be noted.

1) That breathing on a wind instrument is breathing with a difference. When speaking, air is expelled freely, in playing it must be released with care and forethought. Not only has flow to be prolonged, but the control has to be sufficient for alterations of speed to be made en route.

2) To a wind player, the column of air is an extra limb. Unlike string and keyboard players, the person who performs on a recorder employs both hands and lungs.

General points

1. It is better to think of 'breathing' into the recorder than 'blowing' into it. The recorder offers less resistance to the breath-flow than other wind instruments. Forcing the stream forward is not necessary, in fact, air must often be held in reserve to be released as required. People who prefer a hard blow will not be satisfied with the recorder.

2. Despite the above, the breath should have a sense of direction, i.e., be making for some definite point, such as a phrase-end or climax.

Unless breath is carefully managed, pressure will weaken at the end of phrases. The sustaining pedal can come to the aid of the pianist, but a recorder player must keep on working.

Book 1, p.29, no.9

3. Recorder playing and swimming both require breaths to be taken quickly and deeply. On the recorder, drawn in by a wide opening of the throat, as in a whispered 'ah'. Control should come from the diaphragm, not from the top of the lungs.

Breathe through the mouth; through the nose, only during long rests and piano introductions.

4. Listeners should not be aware of the human need for breath, only of the flow of sound. Audible gulps and noisy breathing is never correct, and is always disturbing.

————————————

4. *Hamlet*, Act 3, Scene 2.

Classwork

1.   Single notes can be held without difficulty for twelve or more moderato beats. In 4/4 time a normal breath unit lasts four bars at a moderate count of sixteen beats. In slow tempo, an intake may be necessary after only four beats.

To achieve accurate intonation it is essential that the breath be kept under complete control. Young players enjoy proving their ability: a 'counting clock' can be used.

2.   A sure way to spoil breath control is to play everything Largo. When there are no fingering obstacles, continuity and shape will be improved when speed is increased.

A not unfamiliar request in class is, 'Please may we take it quicker?' If longish phrases are practised as a matter of routine, players learn to imbibe enough air to last out.

Book.1, p.5, no.4

3.   Over-concern about breathing inhibits rather than helps. However, attention should sometimes focus exclusively on the breath, e.g., by repeating the same phrase several times.

4.   Picturesque suggestions will remedy some deficiencies Many strange remarks have done service in this respect.

While in contact with the sound, it is possible to say: 'Press on that note', or 'Make your breath lean forward not backwards'. Nor is it too far-fetched to say, when the pitch drops: 'Don't let your breath drop down to the floor. Make it curl upwards towards the ceiling.'

5.   In the player's mind it does seem that when a tune is properly supported, the jet is directed up, not down; and if pressure slackens, breath does indeed seem to drop.

Playing on the imagination in an instrumental class is as influential as it is in the singing class.

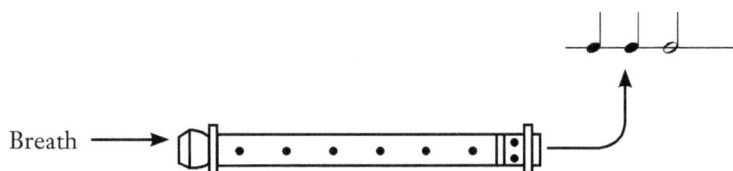

6.   When focussing on the breath, the column of air can be thought of as travelling through the tube, and emerging from the other end.

7. From the first lesson a difference in pupils' aptitude is noticeable. Some take to recorder playing like ducks to water; others find breath control and co-ordination difficult.

The fortunate ones have a natural aptitude, enabling them to 'centre' notes without difficulty, and straightway play in tune; this establishes a standard for the others.

8. When teaching a group, or an individual, it is easier to expand a small sound than to reduce one which is over-robust or tense. Over-blowing can become a persistent problem, once it has set in.

9. Recorder playing differs from singing in one essential: the vibrations which produce the sound are set up <u>after</u> breath has left the mouth. The notes come not from the vocal cords but by the lip of the recorder cutting the air-stream.

10. The equilibrium of a class can be upset by the smallest detail. Physical or mental discomfort has a direct effect on the sound produced. A new room with unfamiliar acoustics, or a change of seating, is enough to cause insecurity and a diminution of tone.

Further examples: (1) standing for a public performance instead of the accustomed seating; (2) playing without sufficient rehearsal in a strange hall; (3) reading from unfamiliar copies; (4) being given too little time to become acclimatised to a different acoustic.

11. Ideally, it is best to alternate sitting and standing during practice sessions. Given a choice, an individual pupil invariably prefers to stand.

A recorder player should stand like the violinist; pressure on one foot; lightly on the other.

12. The advice to a class, 'Always play softly' does not produce warm, satisfying tone, and should not be adopted as a slogan. At the time of a general request to 'play softly', some players in a large group will already be 'under-blowing'.

Common faults

Stuffy rooms are uncomfortable for wind players. Lack of fresh air affects control, especially on public occasions, when an audience uses up air. But some defects are predictable, and can be cured.

1. 'Snatching' and 'bumping' before or after a breath intake is quite common. If the lungs are too full, unevenness is more difficult to avoid. The note following an intake of breath requires special care because breath pressure is strongest at that time. Some notes may sharpen, some even 'explode'.

2. In a group, some members may forget to take a proper breath (or one at all) before starting to play.

3. Misjudging quantities: allowing the breath reserve to be completely used up, necessitating a sudden, and probably noisy, intake.

4. Damaging the musical sense by taking unnecessary breaths. All rests are not breathing places, as is sometimes stated.

etc.

Book.2, p.22, no.10

5. Joins can be potential time-losers. Breaths are taken within the bar, the note before an intake losing some of its duration.

etc.

Book.1, p.35, no.6

6.   Weak breathing results in loss of expression and animation, and must be classed as a fault; good time-keeping alone is not enough.

Editing

1.   In Ensemble Music it matters greatly where breaths are taken. When not printed, breath marks should be added and carefully observed; it is unwise ever to trust to luck. Haphazard or absent-minded breathing weakens the combined tone.

Written breath marks have a secondary function; they serve as visual-aids, enabling players to plan ahead.

2.   The spacing in well-edited music is a guide to its correct tempo. When practising slowly, however, extra breathing places may be needed.

3.   Breath marks aid, but do not make the phrasing. Some confusion exists over this point. Many a breath has to be taken for physical reasons only, and not because of phrasing.

4.   Elementary music tends to be printed either with too many breath marks, or none at all. Too many intakes are not good physically or rhythmically.

5.   An editor should keep in mind that additional breath is used up in *forte* passages, in the higher register, in upward leaps; and that tenors and basses use more breath than descants and sopraninos.

6.   Double bars are accepted as breathing places, so no written breath-marks are required.

7.   In solo music some intakes are big, some small. It may be expedient in long, rapid passages, to snatch one or more quick breaths before reaching the main breathing place.

Different marks can be used:—

V = normal

(V) = optional

v = small, extra intake

V = above-average intake

8.   In group playing momentum and tonal flow are sometimes best achieved by allowing individual breaths to be taken at different times (i.e. 'staggered' breathing).

Vocal influence on recorder playing

Originally, singing was the basis of recorder instruction. Virdung, Agricola and Ganassi all focus attention on the breath, its control, and its vibrant quality. Ganassi's *Method* of 1535 even advocates that the human voice be imitated and a vocal style adopted.

Although this approach may be regarded as extreme, and the outcome of the vocal bias of the time, nevertheless the key to artistry lies in the breath. A closeness between playing and singing will enhance instrumental quality, whilst the player who sings is likely to gain flexibility and insight in interpreting music which has no words.

Two main objectives

1)   To establish a length of breath sufficient to sustain and enliven musical phrases.

2)   For the breath to be pliable enough to remain harnessed to the performer's musical instincts.

6

Playing in tune

Introduction

Intonation is the most crucial part of recorder playing: in the handling of this subject we stand or fall.

Among musicians the topic is a persistent one. Those who dislike the recorder immediately voice two criticisms: (1) The shrill sound of the descant, and (2) that the instrument always plays out of tune.

The charge is disconcerting: what is being criticized is not the instrument, but the way it is played.

At the outset, two ideas need to be reconciled

1.   That the recorder is an easy instrument, possible to learn without much effort.

2.   That 'playing in tune' on the recorder is achievable only after long experience.

The first has commercial value, whilst the second is a convenient ivory tower. If the pessimistic view is adopted, what can be done to make life acoustically tolerable in the meanwhile? Is there one law for singers and another for recorder players?

Quite elementary players will play in tune when this requirement is accepted as normal, and when they are shown how. Good attainment will be achieved if the teacher:—

1.   Teaches the appropriate breath pressure with each new fingering.

2.   Remains alert to individual fluctuations of pitch within the group.

3.   Always rates tonal quality above mere agility.

4.   Aims for a standard well above the lowest common denominator of the class.

The aural approach

This gives quality and significance to each new sound at the time of its introduction. New notes are placed in contexts that help the mind to retain them.

A new note, then, is more than just a different fingering; it is a location in pitch — a distance to be measured from notes already positioned.

Tuning

No aural refinements will succeed unless each instrument is in tune. Promising group-work can be spoilt by hurried or uncompleted tuning. If attention is focused briefly on individual players, others can judge the tone and pitch as it is adjusted.

Method I: Individual Tuning

Each recorder is tuned to a fixed descant 'A' supplied by the teacher,[5] the pitch of the un-tuned instruments being raised or lowered to coincide. When both pitches have merged, the next recorder is tested, and so on quickly round the class.

A further element in the calculation is tone; a change of quality is clearly discernible when the target (the tonal centre) has been reached.

---

5. British Standard Pitch is A = 440 vibrations per second at a temperature of 20° C or 68° F.

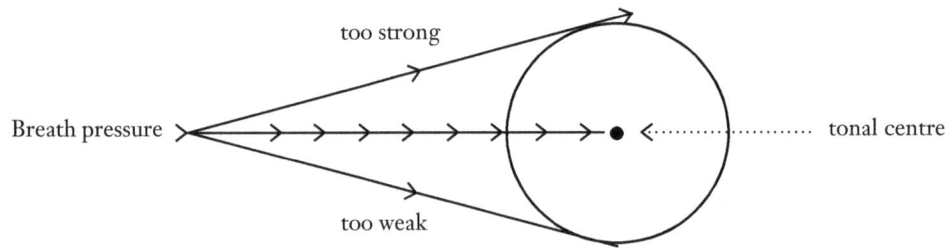

As an exercise in 'aiming', a pupil can be asked to vary breath pressure. Then, after increasing sharpness to the point of discomfort, be asked to return to the tuning level.

When teacher and pupil both over-blow (which may happen in the excitement of the moment) the alignment will not be true, and the sound not have good quality. The notes may be 'in tune', but 'out of tone'.

If pitch is too far out of alignment, the length of the pupil's recorder needs adjusting. A united tuning level should emerge after a few moments of trial and error.

Method II: Tuning in threes

Three recorders are tuned, and blended into a single unit. A series of other players join, one at a time, until the bloc is complete. In each case the new member brings the 'A' into alignment with the group, and not vice versa; thereby narrowing down on defaulters.

Alternatively, several blocs of three can play and be checked together. Despite careful tuning some blocs are surprisingly difficult to match; an indication of the out-of-tuneness which goes undetected, or is tolerated, in normal playing.
N.B. With recorders, 'three's company', while two is not.

Method III: Bloc tuning

Tuning an ensemble *en masse* is a dangerous method, demanding not only an acute ear, but a sixth sense.

The checking of separate blocs of descants, trebles and tenors is just feasible, but works best when a close partnership exists between conductor and players. Misfit instruments must be located quickly, and have their tuning adjusted.

Bulk tuning in public is not safe, unless the instruments have been tuned off-stage, possibly by adopting Sir Henry Wood's method of a march past a fixed 'A'. Unfortunate demonstrations of massed tuning occur at festivals and school concerts, when shortage of time and space causes the conductor to trust in Providence alone.

Systematic tuning is usually abandoned when concert platforms are mounted from the body of a hall. In a moment of nervousness a combined 'A' is requested, the resultant chorus of 'A's being more likely to frighten the Gods than to win their support.

Method IV: 'Handing on'

Starting from a tuned descant, the 'A' is passed along the line from one player to the next (the 'gossip' method). The first and last players compare their versions, the process being repeated until the defaulter is located. A bad unison produces beats (dissonant vibrations) which are an aid to the solving of faulty tuning. One-to-a-part consorts customarily use the 'hand-on and compare' method, the leader giving the first 'A'.

A group that meets regularly, and whose members 'know' their recorders in relation to the others, can quickly tune by the 'handing-on' method.

Further points about tuning

1. Regular ensembles sometimes adopt the short-cut method of tuning descants, trebles and tenors first in units of three, and then together. Those who cause a slight buzz on the pitch float can usually be spotted quickly.

2. The best note for tuning 'F' recorders (sopranino, treble, and bass) is 'D'. The usual pinched 'A' is not reliable; on a treble this note can be particularly chameleon-like.

    The 'A's of the descants and tenors with the 'D's of the trebles and basses make convenient fifths and octaves for tuning and cross-checking. Two fingers plus thumb for all.

3. Tuning mishaps occur at concerts. The conductor must act if disturbance in pitch persists. Players may be aware, but be unable to remedy on their own. At the first opportunity the instrument must be heard, and the correction indicated. If the conductor is unhappy about the tuning of a whole section, (e.g. the trebles), individual players should be heard and adjustments made. Obvious inaccuracies should not be left to remedy themselves.

4. A class of descants should tune to an already tuned descant, and not to the piano. Assuming the teacher's instrument has been warmed, its 'A' should be transferred.

    A tuning fork can be used for the original 'A', but not for tuning individual instruments. Tuning to a violin is even less satisfactory.

Note: Even a tuning fork changes slightly in pitch if the temperature has risen. An electronic tuner is the ultimate in reliability.

5. When there is a pitch disagreement between two 'A's, beats are heard. This aid to tuning occurs within the interval of a second, and disappears when the two merge into a perfect unison.

    Pitch-awareness comes with practice. Some players are lucky: the majority has to acquire discernment. Not easy at first, because of the descant's high pitch, and because sound-vibrations are near the players' ears.

6. To demonstrate pitch discomfort, two 'A's can be dislodged and then returned to consonance. It is a jarring sound that listeners to recorders find so unpleasant.

7. Intonation practice: the 'A' is added in various situations, partly to amuse, but with a serious purpose.

Tuning one recorder

Applying the principle of 'the longer the deeper', a minute lengthening at the head joint alters the pitch. As little as 1/16th of an inch can make a difference.

When the middle joint is pushed in fully, pitch cannot be raised further, except by breath-pressure or room temperature. There can be a semitone difference in pitch between a cold and a warm instrument. *N.B.* Pulling out the head-joint affects the middle register more than the upper or lower registers.

Testing a new recorder

An experienced player wishing to test a selection of descant recorders would:—

1. Judge the basic resistance to breath pressure by playing the middle register notes A, B, (C).
2. Look for unreliable chromatic notes, e.g. F# and C#[1].
3. See whether the three registers blend comfortably.
4. Find out whether the high notes are reachable.
5. Play staccato notes at each register to check on clarity of speaking.

6.   Try some octaves to test for intonation.

    N.B. New wooden recorders need playing-in: between 10–40 minutes for several weeks; they can lose tone if over-played.

1.   Each recorder has a basic breath-pressure. This varies with different makes of instrument: the better the recorder the more balanced the registers.

2.   A player must be prepared to alter breath-pressure when changing instruments. Different resistances may unsettle playing for a time: some recorders are always uncomfortable for some players.

3.   An appreciable adjustment is required when changing from descant to tenor, whether of the same make or not. Tone management is more difficult — the tendency is to under-blow.

    A young player cannot instantly transfer from descant to treble without conscious adjustment. The order of fingers and holes may be the same, but resistance and control differs.

4.   To the teacher aiming at a high standard, choice of instruments is important. Too great an assortment of makes does not produce the best result, as recorders differ in tone and tuning. Ideally, in a class all descants should be the same; a mixture of wooden and plastic trebles may also be difficult to blend.

5.   That recorders do differ is apparent when a consort invites guest players: even recorders of the same make are not identical on every note. It pays to know one's instrument thoroughly, and to avoid sudden changes. It is not wise to keep a set of recorders for "Sunday best", and distribute them before a concert.

6.   It is seldom possible adequately to test a recorder in a music shop: the moment of unpacking is not the moment of truth. Taken from its packaging the instrument is cold, and in need of warmth from hand and breath. Only when 20°C (68° F) has been achieved will pitch settle to its true level.

7.   All recorders do not react uniformly to an increase in temperature. Some plastic makes quickly sharpen, other wood instruments delay at first, and then rise with a jerk. Idiosyncrasies of pitch should be kept in mind when tuning an ensemble of different makes.

8.   Sharpness is a main hazard of public performance. In a hot room a harpsichord may drop in pitch, and the recorders rise.

Recorders with strings and brass can prove troublesome at a concert, because, in varying degrees, all will rise in pitch. Even an organ cannot be relied on always to remain the same, and after a while it may become 'detached' from the other instruments.

Tuning an ensemble

(a)   When a recorder group first assembles it can be a help if combined tuning is postponed until the instruments have settled in. After being played for a time, they will then have warmed and risen in pitch.

N.B. The members of an adult group arrive in varying moods and states of tension. A short settling-in period helps them to forget their worries. Each meeting, in fact, has a prevailing mood, and some of these have an adverse effect on the tuning.

(b)   It is customary for a consort, or small ensemble without piano, to tune to the lowest unalterable pitch.

(c)   A conductor tuning a large group before a public performance must be realistic and ingenious:—

    i)   When instruments are cold, and time is short, it can be wise to tune all slightly flat to allow for a rise in pitch.

    ii)   When dealing with less experienced groups at a public occasion, a small allowance may have to be made when tuning those who over or under-blow due to nerves.

    iii)   There is often some over-blowing in the lower parts of a large ensemble, so tenors and basses can be tuned a fraction below the pitch of the other recorders.

    iv)   It may be that when all recorders are tuned, one remains obstinately flat. If the pitch cannot be raised, a decision must be made: whether to tune all others down, or eliminate the offending instrument. Substitution is best — a wise conductor carries spares.

v) A similar problem arises when an ensemble with one flat instrument is being accompanied by a piano (or organ). When no other solution is possible, it is better to unite the recorders and allow the smallest of gaps between them and the fixed pitch instrument. In a large hall or church such discrepancies can go unnoticed.

Playing in tune with others

Correct intonation on a wind or string instrument implies flexibility. Any single note will be in tune only if it is correctly related to the note preceding and following, and to the note or notes sounding at the same time.

When playing with a fixed-pitch instrument (e.g. piano, harpsichord, or organ) the recorder players' note-pitching must tally as closely as possible. But when free of the restriction, the placing of notes within the octave may be — in fact, has to be — tampered with if the music is to sound perfectly in tune.

There are two adjustments involved, the horizontal (or melodic), and the vertical (or harmonic). The latter is used by experienced choirs and string quartets as a normal part of their work. When the two demands come into conflict, a compromise must be reached. Usually the chord wins, especially when sustained at the end of a phrase or cadence.

As the piano is tuned to equal temperament, all major thirds are slightly too wide. A recorder consort would make them less wide. Octaves would remain the same; thirds and fourths may need to come down, fifths go up.

N.B. Niceties of tuning, such as the above, are only for the experienced. It is not suggested they be widely used.

1. Adult players tend to be less reliable when tuning in public. The sudden spotlight turned on them brings embarrassment, and causes pressure and pitch to be misjudged.

2. With any age-group, interval-tuning makes a change. Various 'A's and 'D's are sample tested, singly or in threes; combined, and varied. The D major chord is built, with the third (F#) added last.

3. Any diatonic chord can be spot-checked, e.g. first and last chords of pieces, and those at cadences. Doubtful intonation during rehearsal may result in a test, followed by a quick re-tune.

   Occasional intonation-plus-tuning practice alerts players to the standard of their contribution, dispelling the feeling that there is safety in numbers.

4. The adjustment of a final chord is crucial; a satisfactory solution can achieve a tonal glow otherwise lost.

5. Every class teacher has an 'impossible' day, when instruments defy tuning. However frustrating the attempts may be, nothing is gained by ill-temper. Although a mutiny is suspected, the cause is probably humidity — simply blame the weather, and wait for it to change.

Intervals

Intonation awareness develops quickly when each interval is felt and cherished. It is customary in singing classes for certain intervals to be rehearsed separately, sometimes with the aid of Tonic Sol Fah (a system that encourages reliable intonation by caring for melodic distances).

The way is thus prepared for the same intervals appearing in vocal music. It is equally apt in recorder teaching. The following points have an influence on the mental gauging of distances: —

a) Positioning is easier when the new interval or note-sequence is presented in a melodic setting previously encountered. In everyone's possession is a mental 'library' of intervals acquired from Nursery Rhymes, Traditional Songs and Hymns; a valuable treasury which should not be ignored.

b) Harmony has a subtle but formative influence on a player's melodic development. Recorder classes, therefore, should have the support of chords; at least for part of the time.

   Self-taught players, cut off from other music-making, fix note-distances to suit themselves. Deprived of harmony, their intonation grows away from that of others.

c)   Intervals are the emotional 'bricks' of music. A player with a feeling for harmony will endow note-relationships with an extra significance.

Alterations of breath pressure

1.   No tune is so simple that breathing and pressure can be ignored. The ability to negotiate an alteration of breath pressure comes as soon as low notes are added to those of the left hand: a skill that includes making breath adjustments for low, middle and high registers.

2.   A player whose breath pressure is weak, secures the lowest notes, under-nourishes the middle ones, and fails to reach the top. A soloist who persistently over-blows, secures the high notes, forces the middle register, and is sharp on the low notes.

3.   The notes F to bottom C require a reduction in breath pressure on the descant, while the notes F^1 to the top take a slight increase. The recorder is made this way: to stay in tune a player must adjust accordingly. In addition, players must accept features peculiar to their own instrument. (Breath adjustments have more effect on the treble recorder because of the greater circumference of note.)

4.   A descant instrument's natural pitch is gauged from the middle notes G to C^1. G resists slightly more than the others. The notes D^1 and E^1 are 'lightweight', and easily 'lift-off'.

Examples:*

Book.1, p.16, no.8

Book.1, p.15, no.7

Book.2, p.4, no.3

N.B. All are approximations.

*Expression marks indicate relative pressure and are not dynamic marks as such.

5.   Intonation suffers when a player presses ahead regardless of the need for flexibility. In example 5, if breath pressure is not eased, the F#s will be above pitch. If even pressure is maintained, some extra finger coverage would be necessary.

(F#=123 / 234 or 123 / 234)

Book.1, p.22, no.23

6.   (a) Breath adjustments become second nature when phrases are carefully repeated as exercises.

        (b) When a large group of descants plays the pentatonic notes B A G E D with sensitive pressure, a marked undulation of tone is heard.

(added)

Book.1, p.15, no.2

7.   When melodies are transposed, all intervals will need to be re-assessed.

Intonation of particular notes

1. One of the secrets of playing in tune is knowing in advance how the instrument will react to the demands made upon it, i.e. what level of pitch the intended notes will achieve. The guide is given as a starting point.

2. A poor recorder can have one or more notes which cannot be absorbed into a normal breath pressure scheme. Even a reputable instrument may have a note requiring careful attention.

3. On a good instrument there must still be awareness of small differences. Such refinements look exacting and even fussy. The aim is not to dishearten, but to assist players to listen, evaluate, and perform musically. The recorder player, like the violinist, is under an obligation to play in tune. Both make their own notes and must be equally sensitive aurally.

4. For the lowest notes it is essential that light tonguing be used, combined with a reduced breath-pressure. Most high notes also succeed with light (if short) tonguing, in addition to an appropriate increase in breath-pressure. Only the highest notes require a strong pressure.

Diatonic

E^1 A 'lightweight' note; soon rises in pitch.

D^1 Can sharpen above *mf* pressure; offers little resistance.
  May need a RH finger added as 'ballast'.

C^1 No trouble, but can be rather harsh in tone.

G Offers slightly more resistance than notes B and A.

F Easy to misjudge at first; can need 'nursing'.

Chromatics

$G\#^1$ Often flat; may need easing up (partially uncover RH.1).

Eb^1 To be treated according to circumstances. (May need : O 123 / 123).

$C\#^1$ A crucial note to test: the worse the instrument, the flatter $C\#^1$.

Bb To reach true pitch usually ₁ ⌒ 3/1 ₃ is needed.

G# Will sharpen above *mp*: (add half LH3.)

F# The other crucial note; easily over-blown (add RH4, or half 4).
  On a poor instrument this note will be out of pitch alignment.

It would be easier if the air-stream could remain constant, but on the recorder this would be disastrous. Like a garden hose, pressure must be increased or slackened to accommodate variants.

Intonation in class

1. Group playing inevitably produces some unwanted variations of breath pressure, from a single player or several at the same time. On hearing these fluctuations it must be decided whether they are errors of the moment, or whether remedial treatment is called for.

2. Pitch can drop through lack of concentration, especially on sustained notes, ties, and at phrase-ends. When some recorders lose pitch, whilst others remain steady, the result is painful to most ears, although the players themselves often remain oblivious.

3. A single interval, or tiny group of notes, is enough to disturb the intonation of an entire phrase. Time is saved when troublesome places are spotted, and dealt with in advance, preventing minor difficulties from turning into chronic ones.

4. Players compete with each other when playing in large numbers, and breath pressures are likely to increase. Members need reminding sometimes that when in company, they should forego a soloistic style of delivery and keep their ears tuned to the players nearest them.

5. Too much playing 'en masse' can be harmful; the less players hear themselves, the more likely they are to play out of tune. Sectional practice lightens the load, allows some to rest, and gives all an opportunity to listen. The more contrapuntal parts there are, the more difficult it is to hear individual discrepancies of intonation.

6. Well-toned, unison playing should come before part-playing, and then be kept up along with other work. Rhythmic life and coherence in music of several parts is achieved by drawing interest from each melodic line. This is so, even when the separate parts appear to have no special interest, e.g. in Chorales, hymns and other music with a straight succession of chords. Intervals are always of interest.

Intonation of a recorder consort

While equal temperament is essential for keyboard instruments (whose pitch cannot be governed at will by the player, and must be adhered to by recorder players when being accompanied) the recorder consort, in common with the string quartet and an *a Cappella* choir, is free to use untempered intervals in any key.

For example: the player holding the major third in a common chord will increase the sweetness of the chord by slightly flattening the pitch; a similar effect is achieved when a minor third is widened in pitch. The fifth need no longer be flattened, but may be widened into the true interval; and the player holding the fourth may lower it slightly to make it true.

There is freedom to raise leading notes slightly; with some expressive gain in doing so. But octaves should always remain true and unaltered.

7

Tone and vibrato

Tone in class

1. Good tone, a player's greatest asset, is easier to demonstrate than to write about. Closely linked to intonation, tone loses quality when notes move away from the true centre of pitch.

    a) In a group, extra resonance is achieved by unanimity of tone.

    b) Such is the effect of good tone that a small group can sound much larger.

    c) Hear good tone and you believe in it.

2. Good tone need not be sacrificed when a group of recorders play in unison, if notes are threaded through their pitch-centre. However, a mixture of wood and plastic is a handicap.

3. Interval coaching in small numbers pays dividends. Short solos also play a part, with those with the best tone being used as models.

4. Loose lips and a relaxed throat contribute to a 'round' tone — the throat cavity widening as in a whispered 'Ah'.

5. A relaxed tongue is essential for good tone production; if the tongue is not free the throat will tighten.

6. Repeating phrases at different intensities, with a request to 'warm the sound', helps to avoid the dull playing which too often spoils performances of recorder music.

7. Blowing harder when asked to improve tone is self-defeating. Over-blown notes contain impurities that make the sound project less well.

8. Tone is a personal quality; as people are so they play. Different players make the same music sound different. Adult players in particular, may identify too closely with their instrument, giving an over-subjective interpretation to all their music-making.

    Behaviour reveals personality, so it is possible to tell whether a player is inhibited, over-confident, or tense. One individualistic player can spoil the sound of a whole class.

9. Duration, pitch, volume, and speed are printed in the copies; what is not shown is the appropriate tone to be added. This vital element is left to the experience and artistic judgement of the performer.

10. Acoustic environment affects performance. Over-resonance flatters, and under-resonance impoverishes. A degree of resonance is essential: players need to hear their tone in order to assess and control it.

    Regular practising in dry, absorbent conditions at home leaves its mark on a player's tone. The sitting-room is not always the best location.

11. Physical or mental discomfort makes players nervous, which dwarfs tone. When circumstances prevent total concentration even a well-trained group can lose its animation. In public performance the margin between success and failure is very small.

12. Seating can be decisive. Good tone quality is difficult to achieve if a group is set too far apart, or at an uncomfortable distance from the piano.

    Outdoor conditions are the most difficult; tone disperses altogether. To be badly positioned for sound and vision is a disturbing experience, the more so if the players' plight is disregarded.

13. Recorder music is graded mostly according to key-signature, fingering difficulty, and ornamentation. Breathing and tonguing are rarely included. The average player is unlikely to say: "I never breathe well in this piece," or "My tone-colour is not up to standard here."

Vibrato

Vibrato animates tone. Pressure variations, riding on the breath, create minute alterations in pitch, above and below the 'plumb-line'.

When singing, many add vibrato naturally. For example, a solo choirboy might need no more encouragement than an example to copy.

The aspirate 'h' is added into the flow of breath, on a long note. Slowly at first, then quickened into a continuous stream. Long notes without vibrato should also be practised. In vibrato, pitch fluctuates slightly above and below the central line known as 'true'.

Vibrato 'warming' is not restricted to sustained notes, but a start can be made with these. Then perhaps be added to each note of a slow scale: an open throat for *Forte*, with a narrower opening for *Piano*.

1. The expressive addition of vibrato is especially appropriate at the peaks of phrases, and at moments of repose during repeating patterns; when an unanimated note would be conspicuous by its plainness.

Long sustained notes need a feeling of growth, particularly when held over moving harmonies. All but the shortest notes, do, in fact, have a beginning, a middle, and an end.

2. Tone does not sound the same to a player as it does to others; vibrato also sounds different. When an uncontrolled tremolo is causing discomfort to others, the player's best friend may not like to comment, but the teacher should.

3. The vibrato of the self-taught is seldom fully controlled. A chronic 'shaker' must be helped for the sake of all. In a school class, vibrating tone is best kept to a minimum, as beats destroy the purity of intonation.

4. An advanced player will sometimes resort to a wide vibrato to disguise a short spell of off-centre playing.

5. An adult's vibrato is, at first, either overdone, or non-existent. On the other hand, musical pupils at school can produce an instinctive vibrato from spontaneous enjoyment of the music.

6. A few types of players in a recorder class: —
    a) Senior pupils tend to over-animate and stress, partly because they sing in choirs and play other instruments.
    b) Adult amateurs, when they first join a class, may not breathe properly, and can be weak on co-ordination and timing.
    c) Music students read music easily, but do not always listen. Surprisingly, if un-curbed they play in a colourless manner.

Conclusion

In breathing, the two main objectives are: —

1. To establish a length of breath sufficient to sustain and enliven the musical phrases.
2. For the breath to be sensitive enough to remain harnessed to the performer's musical instincts.

For group work it is essential to have the right instruments, united in pitch, blended in tone, playing with similar breath pressure and musical intention. Teachers and conductors are then able to adjust, manipulate, and refine the individual and combined characteristics to their own satisfaction. Working on the sound made by a group of players is demanding, but stimulating.

8

Beginner faults

Introduction

Every recorder group has within it one member whose posture is imperfect, or whose technique has an insecure foundation. The faults are frequently of long standing, and not quickly remedied.

A new class gives a teacher a golden opportunity to anticipate the faults of future playing. Some teachers find a Beginners' Class the most stimulating, for it is at this stage that demand on them is the greatest. Optimistically then, the various errors are termed: "Beginner Faults".

Putting the recorder too far into the mouth

1. Beginners are often wet players. A recorder pushed too far into the mouth both increases saliva and makes it more difficult to control. All wind players must remember to swallow. 'Give a man a small flute,' it is said, 'and he will irrigate the Sahara'.

2. Some mouthpieces are too thick for young people, and in addition to moisture trouble, the throat and tongue become tense. Mouthpieces which are too thin are not much better, since they slide too easily into the mouth, and saliva runs down the recorder tube like a dental suction. A plastic recorder absorbs no moisture.

3. Recorder sucking, not uncommon with children, increases the moisture problem. Only the tip of the mouthpiece should rest on the lower lip: the right thumb is there to support.

4. A cold recorder produces the most condensation. The blow-through before a solo is not an affectation, but a practical way of warming the instrument, thereby lowering its moisture potential.

Some players prefer not to blow down the recorder, but to suck moisture back through the mouthpiece. Whichever method is adopted, it is imperative for the lip of the recorder to remain untouched, as oil from the fingers affects this vital air-cutter.

Biting the mouthpiece

Players with a 'lollipop' approach to the mouthpiece usually bite it as well. Teeth marks (and scratches) are frequently found on both plastic and wooden recorders. Always a bad sign: it suggests incorrect posture, faulty tone-production, or agitation, and is probably the result of an oversight by the first teacher.

Hands reversed

1. Young players can forget which hand is placed uppermost. While forgetfulness is excusable once or twice, it is not good to have it repeated often. Those who continue are usually the less able.

2. Despite historical evidence of left-handed recorder playing in early paintings, the class teacher should — except in special cases — see that all left hands are at the top.

A lookout should be kept for reversing, keeping in mind that a complete beginner could misinterpret, through seeing the teacher demonstrate in reverse.

Left hand crooked, i.e. not at right-angles to the recorder

a) If the left hand is allowed to slant, with its little finger too far from the recorder, the other fingers will work less efficiently. (On the treble and tenor LH3. is even less secure if there is a twist in the hand.)

b) Should the first finger knuckle-joint be allowed to press against the recorder, the thumb will also press; and together they will restrict freedom of movement.

Misplacing the right hand, whilst playing with the left hand alone

(1)   This is a true beginner fault. New pupils instinctively clasp the foot joint with their spare hand: they are afraid of dropping the recorder. However, the right hand is essential to a proper hold, and should not be spare.

The trouble is less likely if the supporting role of the right thumb is made clear at the outset. As soon as possible, attempts should be made to cover the right hand holes, and to play a low note on its own.

(2)   If the recorder is unpacked in class, it should first be held vertically in the right hand, like a candle. Then with mouthpiece resting on the chin, the left hand fingers should be positioned and exercised; followed by the right, (the right hand thumb giving support throughout).

This is the opposite approach to that which says: "You are going to learn the left hand notes first, so the right hand is not needed yet."

(3)   It is best to hold the recorder slightly higher than the forty-five degrees usually prescribed: held too low, the recorder tends to slip through the fingers.

Perpendicular fingers

Fingers are kept flatter on the recorder than on the violin, or the piano. Many beginners find the idea unusual, and prefer to have their fingers upright. But fingertips cannot be relied on to keep holes air-tight on treble or tenor, or even on a descant. So the rule is:— 'pads not tips'. *N.B.* If wrists are raised, inevitably fingers rise.

Flat thumbs: protruding right thumb

Fingers are less flexible when thumbs protrude. Thumb trouble is common amongst self-taught players.

Wrists need to drop to allow both thumbs to remain slightly hooked. As the left thumb is used in pinching, it must remain relaxed. In advanced playing the left thumb controls the pitch of high notes by widening or narrowing the aperture. Without a freely moving thumb this manoeuvre is not possible.

Little fingers tucked under

The little fingers of both hands should remain 'above-board'. When either is tucked under, free hand movement is restricted. LH4 is not used for playing; RH4 is. Occasionally it has a further use. If the tip of RH4 is placed on the foot joint moulding, it acts as a steadier, e.g. for the descant trill on C^1.

N.B.

(1)   An adjustable foot-joint must be set to suit the length of the little finger.

(2)   Recorders made in two sections have bottom twin-holes, which do not suit all right hands. Such instruments are not recommended, and if they do appear, should be changed.

'Shooting fingers': raising them in the air while playing

Over-activity of the fingers is not correct. In a beginner, it suggests a lack of physical aptitude. Periodically all players should check their fingers. The mind, or the nerves, may be over-reacting; both can be the cause of fingers 'jumping' or stiffening.

The further the fingers go into the air, the further the journey back; returning from a distance they tend to hit the holes. About half an inch is a reasonable height.

Misjudging breath pressure

Over-blowing is more common than under-blowing, but the latter does exist, and is sure to be found somewhere during the first lessons. Shy, timid players need to be spotted quickly; they do as much damage as the robust ones.

Forgetting to take a breath before playing

This results from absentmindedness or lack of method. To a non-player this may sound curious, but it is a familiar failing with recorder classes, at all levels. The tendency to 'sleep-in' and give a sudden gulp can become a habit, unless breath-taking before an entry is part of normal discipline.

It is best for the preparatory breathe-in to be taken on a pre-arranged beat. Physical discomfort and musical unevenness can result from a first breath being in excess of requirements. Some young players also raise their shoulders. Printed information misleads when it says that lungs should be filled to capacity at each intake.

Over-tonguing, and not tonguing

Starting each note with an explosive 'T' can become a habit. Fortunately the audible click is less common with school groups, but during the first lessons the other extreme may occur, i.e. not tonguing at all; by starting each note with a puff of breath instead of a tongue movement.

Not tonguing the ends of notes

That is, stopping sounds with the breath instead of the tongue. The tongue is the silence-maker, and after allowing the breath to pass, the tongue-tip should return to the hard palate. The clean cutting-off gives the note its 'tonal-edge'.

Being tense and stiff-jointed; playing with a gripped throat and tongue

The habit of tenseness can be troublesome. Playing conditions, music-reading difficulties, and other unhelpful circumstances can cause mental and physical tension, but the most common cause is personal anxiety and nervousness.

Muscular stiffness impedes progress in quick music, but is less noticeable when tempo is slow. Naturally, a tense throat has a damaging effect on tone production.

Drooping: allowing the foot joint to drop out of sight

Class members take up many postures. The correct position for sitting should be shown from time to time, with reminders about keeping a straight back, and not crossing the legs. The recorder is held at about an angle of forty-five degrees to the floor.

Music propped on tables causes slouching. Music stands may need to be adjusted, whether the players are sitting or standing. Two players per stand should be the maximum.

9

The piano

Its value

Whether or not to use the piano at all in recorder teaching is a vexed question. Naturally, those who cannot play the piano claim that it is superfluous, even damaging; yet well used it can be invaluable.

What better partner than one that can play more softly than a recorder, and still be as dynamic and sonorous as the music requires. Besides this, the piano produces instant harmony, in a sustained or a percussive manner, and is an ideal instrument for 'aiding and abetting' the rhythmic and expressive life of the recorder.

Certainly, it is not healthy for a recorder class to be entirely piano-orientated, but neither is it musically healthy for it to exist in a vacuum. Recorder players without a feeling for chords, their progressions, tensions and resolutions, are unlikely to gauge melodic distances sufficiently well to play in tune, either alone or in company with others.

The guitar

The guitar, an alternative to the piano, is admirable in some ways, but it is susceptible to climatic conditions, and requires regular tuning. The piano is not only a more versatile companion, it offers permanent anchorage for pitch and tuning.

Use or abuse?

A school piano is an impersonal piece of furniture, taken for granted and often inconveniently situated. It is easy to lose respect for this long-suffering instrument, and play it less carefully than in home conditions.

Used with a class, the piano should be played neither too much, nor too little, and not too loudly. Special care is always necessary when accompanying recorders. The size of room or hall, the number of players, their proximity to the piano are all factors to be considered; in addition to the mood and style of the music.

The problem of acoustics

Over-resonant school halls, whilst flattering the sound of recorders, can also be detrimental to their welfare. With sound amplified, the piano is encouraged to dominate the weaker instruments. School choirs also suffer, but they can fight back by increasing volume!

It is a sobering thought that many recorder classes must have suffered permanent damage from the over-playing of school pianos. Volume is increased when an upright piano stands away from the wall.

A blanket or soft drape hung over the back of an upright piano might sound unusual, but it does subdue the sound. Householders would not tolerate for long their piano being played in an empty, unfurnished room.

Seating

A compact formation of recorder players, with two to a stand, should sit as close to the piano as is comfortable. This arrangement assists both sound and human contact. Whether sitting or standing, if players curve slightly in horse-shoe fashion, vision also becomes easier. In a large group this arrangement allows the pianist to be visible in gaps between the stands.

Manner of keyboard playing

1. The style to adopt is non-soloistic; more incisive than normal, especially when accompanying a solo recorder. Care is needed to avoid flooding the sound with too much use of the sustaining pedal.
2. When accompanying recorders a pianist should, as a rule, give more weight to the left hand than to the right. Indeed, the left hand must often (especially in 18th-century sonatas) act as a substitute cello. A *cantabile* bass line gives treble instruments a stable foundation.

The combined 'weight' of a group of descants is quite considerable. For the piano to reinforce this bulk at the expense of the harmonic bass notes, would distort the balance. The right hand should not compete with the melody line, but provide the middle part of a three-tier texture — a manner of playing not natural to a pianist accustomed to leaning on the right hand.

3.   Normally, the piano right hand should not stray too far up the keyboard, as recorders seem to sound an octave below their actual pitch.

When a piano plays above treble C^1 it seems to the ear to be not in unison with the descant sound, but actually higher. In modern music a colouristic effect may be intended, but even then it should be handled with care.

4.   A thick piano accompaniment overloads the texture and impedes rhythm. Even with a large group, a low-lying bass below thick chords, is not good. Octaves, in either hand, are best employed for short spells only.

5.   Teacher-pianists with a feeling for textural lightness and simplicity will find some printed music too thick, and not wholly appropriate to their needs. Time given to modification is well spent.

Class Teaching

1.   Part of the pianist's job is to reduce sluggishness. Tonal accents, additional silences, and crisp chording is speech without words. The non-verbal contact can have a marked effect on a group familiar with this mode of communication.

2.   The piano is also a valuable means of illustrating points of interpretation. Piano introductions and interludes tell a group much about rhythm and style without a word being spoken. A few bars in correct tempo makes unnecessary the habit of counting aloud before the recorders' entry — a luxury not possible at a public performance.

3.   The pianist, occasionally, must be able to play with head turned towards the players; an accomplishment that enables visual messages to be sent via the eyes. In an emergency — for a few bars — the bass line could be played an octave higher.

4.   In accompanied music, conducting signals are given from the keyboard. These should be consistent and neat, e.g. a small cutting action to accomplish a release. With careful use of hand signals and other discreet movements, a reciprocal understanding can be established, akin to radar, or so it seems to the observer.

5.   Seated at the piano, teachers are virtually on a rostrum: from this position they hold the reins, and should expect to be watched and listened to; both playing and conducting, and talking takes place from this focal point.

6.   Alternative focal points are the conductor's music stand, and a music whiteboard. If the teacher sits slightly raised when conducting the class, the line of vision is improved. From a sitting position a feeling of intimacy is created, which players appreciate.

If teachers stand, with the focal point too near the front row, they tower above their players like a giant among Lilliputians.

7.   Although a class likes to hear harmonic progressions, and the rhythmic tread of chords, it ought not to have them all the time. The value of the piano is enhanced when part of each session is spent without accompaniment. Learning to keep strict time without support from an external time-keeper is an important part of instrumental training.

OLD MACDONALD

① Slow   Rec.

Book 1, p.27, no.12

② Presto   Rec.

Book 2, p.5, no.6

③ With a swing Rec.

Book 2, p.16, no.7

④ Con brio   Rec.

etc.

Book 2, p.6, no.9

⑤ Boldly   Rec.

Book 2, p.12, no.10

⑥   Rec.

Pianistic devices

1.   Variety and contrast are essential elements in class piano playing. Not every pianist can improvise their own accompaniments, but all can attempt a varied treatment of the printed music. Surprise stimulates young players, whether it be musical sounds, or personal behaviour.

There are various ways of introducing variety for short-term effect:

(1)   Light octave playing high in the treble clef.

(2)   Playing the tune in both hands, an octave apart.

(3)   Introducing melodic variants, or by adding a counter-melody, above or below the main tune; as in a vocal descant.

(4)   Adding rhythmic patterns derived from the recorder part.

(5)   Remaining silent when a phrase repeats.

(6)   Leaving one line of a hymn or other tune unaccompanied.

(7)   For a short time playing both hands an octave higher than printed (breaking the normal rule concerning registers).

(8)   Changing the harmony, momentarily or for a few bars.

(9)   Transferring the treble line to the bass, i.e. reversing the hands.

Entries: securing a good attack

1. A silence following introductory bars (or a single chord) can be relied on as a controlling signal. Both music and silence must keep the same strict pulse. The National Anthem is sometimes started from a chord, plus a silence; thereby dispensing with the traditional drum roll.

2. A united attack can be achieved by ending piano introductions with a rhythmic 'kick'. After some practice, recorder and piano will be able to synchronize without a keyboard accent.

Deputizing role

The pianist's right hand can successfully play the music of a missing treble instrument. For example: played an octave above the treble clef, and in brittle style, a xylophone or chime bar part can sound quite well.

Conclusion

The piano plays a dual role. It controls the musical discipline, and contributes to the emotional life of the class. Since its attributes are both functional and artistic, it is difficult to see how it can be dispensed with.

An average pianist, with just simple chords, can add harmonic interest to any high-altitude musical line.

An able keyboard player can contribute in a more creative way by introducing varied chords, patterns, and colour effects.

By adding vitality and rhythmic support, the piano can enhance the life of that popular, small pipe — the English Flute.

10

Optional percussion

Introduction

The reason for adding solo percussion to recorders is not always understood, and some prejudice needs to be overcome.

To exclude entirely the rhythmic aid of simple percussion appears short-sighted. In a music class all elements go into the melting pot: time, rhythm, notation, form, phrasing, and expression all being dealt with. It is hardly possible to keep them apart.

By simple means, pulse can be heightened, the range of sounds increased, and instrumentation made more interesting. Provided discipline is maintained, the scope of teaching can be widened considerably.

Good use of a small drum aids pulse-awareness. The beat is given a physical presence which, when removed is recalled in the memory. The stronger the feeling of pulse, the better the muscular co-ordination.

The instruments

For selection, one or more of the following:

Hand drum; small drum (using a variety of sticks); tambourine; small triangle, or larger solo triangle; Indian bells; solo cymbal (held, or hung on a music stand).

The following can be added for occasional use; played singly, not all together:

Chime bars, xylophone; glockenspiel.

Benefits

1. The light playing of a hand drum will reinforce pulse without upsetting the general volume.

1. Fairly Quick

drum — Book.1, p.35, no.7

2. Slowly

drum — Book.1, p.32, no.11

2.   When interest is flagging, ancilliary percussion can act as a social tonic. There is never a shortage of volunteers; eagerness is such that the new instruments may need apportioning by rote.

3.   A hand drum or tambourine, played *extempore* by the teacher facing the group, gives the piano a rest.

4.   Varied instrumentation appeals to young people. The selective use of percussion sharpens their wits, and expands class material into what they call 'real music'.

Safeguards

1.   Success is dependent on good discipline. All who have encountered an unruly cymbal player, or faced a fidgety row of tambourines will know that control is essential.

2.   It is necessary to differentiate between untuned percussion (i.e. drum, tambourine, etc.) and tuned percussion (chimes, glockenspiel, etc.). Although classed as melodic, the 'tuned' are not all suited to melody making with recorders.

Phrases on resonating instruments can smudge and blur; better to play individual bell-like notes, unless music is specially composed for tuned percussion. Simple chord patterns, read from guitar letters, work well. The xylophone is more adaptable, and can be used to play tunes, or chords.

3.   Quantity of sound calls for judgement, and discretion. In a quiet setting a large triangle can sound like a fire alarm, and a drum resemble a canon.

Note: Some drums, listed as 'untuned', do in fact play notes of definite pitch, which spoils the recorder sound.

4.   Obviously, the best sound comes from the best instruments; those found in a school cupboard are sometimes best left there.

Practicalities

1.   The percussion playing must be sensitive, with an assortment of beaters, and a range of effects employed. Volume starts from the quietest sound possible on each instrument; any increase being dictated by the demands of the music itself.

2.   One loud player can make all others loud, as can happen with talking during school meals.

3.   Any instrument re-joining the group must be prepared to adapt. Under school conditions numbers fluctuate, changing the balance, and necessitating an adjustment of dynamics.

4.   The ability to remain silent when not playing is a priority: the hall-mark of a good percussionist. This includes all rests and final notes.

Good posture contributes to control. Movement should be positive, yet relaxed, much of the action coming from the wrist and hand.

5.   The percussion players need not be segregated. A solo player sitting or standing near a recorder player can benefit both, the closeness also being a restraining influence. If percussion patterns are added to the recorder copy, one music stand will serve both players.

Recorder players themselves may play percussion for part of the time. With some ingenuity, this is quite possible.

6.   In a regular, well-ordered class, the smaller percussion instruments can rest under chairs, having been distributed before the session. Spare instruments should remain accessible, perhaps on a table near the piano.

The reason given for excluding percussion from music-making is 'practical difficulties'; seldom valid, as most difficulties in school are surmountable.

7.   Basic rhythmic patterns are usually taught by rote, but a selection can be written on the board, for solo or *tutti* playing. Shared out between several instruments, a few simple rhythms will produce a pleasing effect. Successful combinations can always be noted down for use on subsequent occasions.

Traditional Patterns

Book 2, p.13, no.13
And see Book 2, p.18, no.16

'Orchestration'

This takes pattern-playing a stage further. The treatment is more flexible, the instruments used more varied. There are still periods of silence, but *Tuttis* are fuller, and repeats, answering phrases, and cadences are given varied treatment.

In some pieces, patterns can be drawn direct from the music being played.

Pulse playing

Giving pulse a physical existence helps a player to keep steady time, and be accurate over time-divisions. With all but the musically gifted, the instinct needs fostering. A gentle drum tap represents pulse which, when it stops, continues to be heard in the mind. Normally, pulse playing is limited to a single percussion instrument handled with restraint.

Book.1, p.11, no.7

Pattern playing

The rhythmic units chosen for repetition are drawn from the music selected for performance.

N.B. Percussion to be added only in suitable pieces. A tambourine can successfully play from a tenor recorder copy, if appropriate rhythmic patterns are chosen.

Basic patterns are customarily taught by rote, but a selection can be written on the whiteboard and used for solo or *tutti* playing. Shared between several percussion instruments, a few patterns can create a pleasing instrumentation. Successful combinations can be noted down for use on subsequent occasions.

Creative playing

Extempore playing in class may be a frightening prospect, but it has its place. Some music lends itself to the addition of free percussion, imaginatively employed.

Freedom to enjoy can bring confidence, and a willingness to be disciplined. The atmosphere should be one of discovery and inventiveness.

The musical horizon

In combined music-making several practical and aesthetic points arise, which link the most modest classroom effort with the world of music outside. They include:

1. Finding an appropriate style for each piece.
2. Being unselfish, whether as accompanist or soloist.
3. Following the rule of 'give and take'.
4. Remaining resilient and alive; not repeating the same notes in the same way each time.
5. Realizing the importance of rhythm as opposed to metre.
6. Developing an analytic approach, both to performance and to the sounds themselves.

Conclusion

Provided combined playing is not too frequent, both recorders and percussion gain from the partnership. The recorder players' rhythmic sense will increase, and the percussion will play more musically through contact with melody.

The introduction of varied timbres and rhythmic elements can improve the musicality of a class. Individual members benefit from switching to instruments easier to play than the recorder: and the making of music can become more absorbing and enjoyable for everyone.

Appendix

Rhythm

1. Too many 'on-the-beat' accents reinforce metre at the expense of rhythm. In interpretation, the concept of anacrusis is important; particularly the lift-off at the beginning of a tune, ex. 1, 2, and 3.

Not confined to first entries, the manner of handling this factor contributes to a forward rhythm in phrasing.

2. Beware the tyranny of the bar-line. The lines are there to mark off the measures; they can so easily spoil musical sense, and induce breaks in continuity.

3. Young players can usually assimilate tricky rhythms best when they are presented first on a single note. Fingering uncertainties do, of course, cause slow-downs, but rhythmic units and time-divisions can also impede progress.

4. Speech is a natural aid to rhythm and good phrasing. Verbal emphasis illustrates accentuation and shape better than lengthy explanation.

References to physical movement is appropriate; to 'a flowing style'; 'moving gracefully'; 'dancing on the tips of the toes'; — the opposite to 'dancing in hob-nail boots'.

It has been said that rhythm is the life-blood of music. Certainly, a performance which has rhythmic life, propulsion, and continuity is noticeably superior to one which has only accuracy of notes and time.

Class teaching

1.   Group teaching has many advantages: more scope for variety; for making comparisons, for stimulating interest, and, in school, for being able to draw on the competitive instinct natural to the young.

2.   The additional volume is not a handicap when the tonal bulk is divided into smaller units. While one group plays the others do 'silent drill', i.e. fingering without the sound. Listening to others and making judgements is part of the exercise.

3.   Pupils will probably themselves learn new notes. To recognise their initiative, the progressive ones can perform in class the tunes learnt at home.

4.   One small difficulty can upset a phrase several bars long. The troublesome interval, or finger movement, should be isolated for thoughtful repetition, and then returned to its setting.

Almost every piece has some difficulty the players themselves would like to repeat.

5.   That an unsuitable choice of music can actually impede progress is a fact of life. All new repertoire should be carefully assessed for instrumental suitability, with a watch kept for time-divisions and rhythms more advanced than the stage reached.

6.   A private 'concert' for the Head Teacher, or an unexpected visitor, tests the nerves and indicates the overall standard attained. It also marks a point on the graph of advancement, which permanent rehearsing does not.

Conclusion

The best recorder teaching takes account of the pupils' aural task, and accepts that, in addition to controlling bodily actions, each must learn to listen with the physical and 'inner' ear; a proficiency acquired mainly in lesson time.

To the enlightened teacher, music is a language as well as a skill, and because all performance communicates, the emotions are involved. In consequence, tone, colour, and blend are essential qualities which cannot be bypassed. The goal for both pupil and teacher is the same; not physical dexterity alone, but genuine artistic fulfilment.

Scales as Intonation exercises for descant recorder

Play slowly at first, concentrating on pitch and tone.
The marks are breath-pressure equivalents, not dynamic marks.

*Finger-pressure on the B helps to carry the fingers over the C#¹ 'hump'.

Scales (Rhythmic)

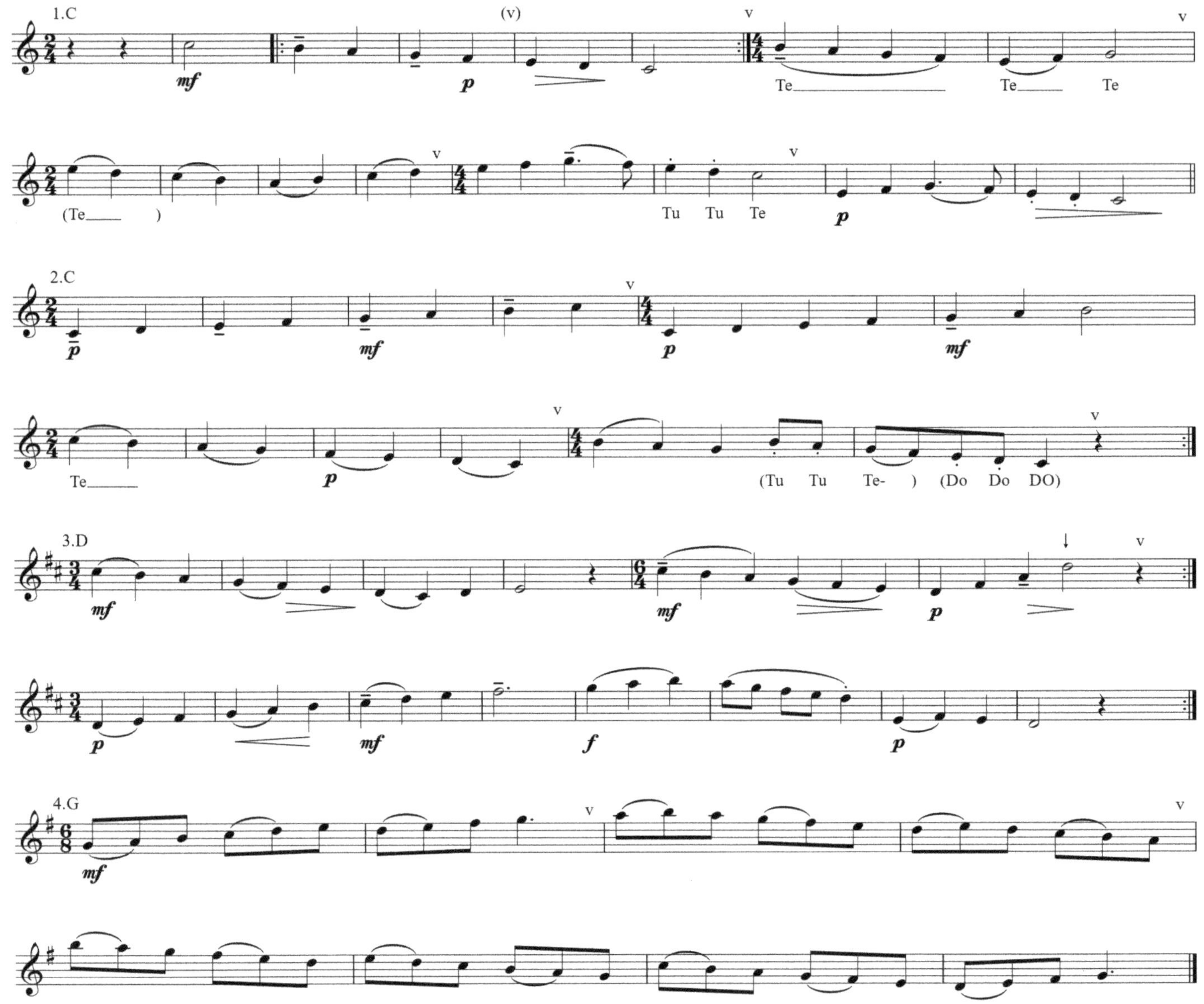
1.C
Te
Te
Te
(Te)
Tu Tu Te
2.C
Te
(Tu Tu Te-) (Do Do DO)
3.D
4.G

Scales (Intonation) continued

Care and Maintenance

Before play

Blow through the recorder for a moment or two, keeping a finger over the window. This helps the pitch to settle. Condensation can be reduced by warming the instrument in the hands. A screwing movement should be adopted when the sections are being joined or separated. Avoid pushing and pulling, and always turn in the same direction.

During play

A new recorder should be played-in for short spells, building up to not more than half-an-hour. An occasional sharp blow through clears any moisture. The drier the mouth the less saliva will escape into the instrument. It is important that the mouthpiece rests on the lips, and is not pushed into the mouth.

After play

Take the sections apart, and wipe by pulling a rolled silk handkerchief or soft rag through the bore. Soft woollen mops are not recommended because they shed fibres. They can have a use, however, in helping to move material through the individual sections. Be careful that nothing hard is pushed against the lip. The windway can be cleared with a feather. The after-play clean applies equally to plastic and wooden recorders.

Between play

Attend to the joints. Too slack can affect pitch, or cause the foot to drop off; too tight can cause a crack. To correct looseness, moisten the cork rings, or use a small amount of transparent adhesive tape. For stiffness, lubricate cork with lanolin, paraffin grease, or similar. 'Vaseline'™ is not suitable. If joint is lapped with thread, apply beeswax or candle wax.

After care

If the bore of a wooden recorder is unvarnished, oil about every three months with a cloth impregnated with raw linseed or almond oil, the latter is also good for the outside. Warm the bottle of oil in the hands before use. Wipe off surface oil with a clean cloth. The windway should not be oiled. Use cotton wool to remove dirt from finger holes. Plastic recorders should also be kept clean, inside and out, using warm water with a few drops of 'Milton'™ added.

Borrowing recorders

The borrowing and lending of recorders is not advisable for health reasons. Infection can be spread via the mouthpiece: the risks include the common cold, mouth infections, herpes, in addition to the more serious complaints of influenza and food poisoning. If necessary, sterilize the head of the recorder using sterilizing tablets that are readily obtainable at pharmacies.

Storing

To allow the sections to dry, keep them apart. Store in an open case in a cool temperature, away from dust. Wooden recorders, especially, should be kept away from fires and radiators.

Repair

The thumb-hole needs re-bushing when the wood becomes dented with frequent use. A metal or ivory ring is inserted; a repair for a professional, along with the periodic re-voicing of hand-made recorders.

Biographical Note

Robert Salkeld, Hon. FLCM, ARCM, was born on 16 April 1920 at Newcastle-upon-Tyne. He was educated at Ascham House Preparatory School, the Royal Grammar School in that city, Newcastle Conservatoire of Music, and after wartime military service, at the Royal College of Music (1947–49) where in addition to piano and viola he studied composition, harmony and counterpoint with R. O. Morris (1886–1948).

On graduation he combined three years of full-time teaching as Head of Music at Collingwood School, Peckham, London, with playing the harpsichord, viola, and recorder with various ensembles and performers including Carl Dolmetsch, Joseph Saxby, Walter Bergmann, Edgar Hunt, and Layton Ring. From then on his musical career was entirely free-lance.

From 1950–69 Salkeld was a Senior Tutor at Morley College and Director of the Morley College Recorder Consort, which had a full and varied performance programme in the capital. From 1961–69 he was Professor of Recorder at the London College of Music, which from 1964 had as its Director, Dr. William Lloyd Webber who brought in the "Golden Age" of the College; Salkeld was made an Honorary Fellow of the LCM in 1977 and was a Senior Examiner until 1982. He combined these appointments with teaching positions in schools (1949–69), and from 1949–72, extensive work at competitive music festivals, summer schools and courses including at Toynbee Hall, and in 1962 at Woolley Hall, West Riding of Yorkshire, whose Warden, Diana Jordan OBE, was a leading authority on movement/dance (Laban) in education, and at Lady Mabel College, Wentworth Woodhouse (see illustration, p. 58). He contributed reviews to "Music in Education" from 1954–76.

Publications: Concert Pieces, 1951, *Play the Recorder Series* (1966), Chester Recorder Series (1970); editions include Byrd, Weldon, Valentine, Arne, Hook etc. Publishers: Faber, Schott and Universal Edition. His many unpublished compositions are held at the University of Cambridge | Library, Special Collections.

Salkeld's entry in *International Who's Who in Music* where he describes himself as "teacher, examiner, and editor" ran from the mid-1950s until the 2007 edition, the last edition before his death at Peebles, Scottish Borders, in 2011. He put the finishing touches to his *Teach the Recorder: A Companion to the 'Play the Recorder'* Series in 2008.

For a full account see 'John Turner on the life of Robert Salkeld' in "Recorder Magazine", Autumn 2012, pp. 97–99.

COUNTY COUNCIL OF THE WEST RIDING OF
YORKSHIRE EDUCATION COMMITTEE

Woolley Hall

Woolley, near Wakefield   Darton 238

Warden Miss D. Jordan

8.12.62.

Dear Mr Salkeld,

This is just to send you our
warmest thanks for all your help on the Music Course.
The "advanced" recorder group certainly gained in
quality and in confidence if one can judge by the way
they played at the end and I am sure this <u>was</u> evidence.

I hope you enjoyed it as much as I know they did —
But over and above your professional gift to the
Course, we just enjoyed having you with us!
"Woolley" hopes to see you again when, as we hope,
we shall have another lively weekend —

Miss Spence recovered from her cold, but Mr Gavall
has been in bed, and I only hope that you haven't been
a victim which would be rude treatment indeed from
the West Riding!

Again many thanks.

Yours sincerely

[*signed*] *Diana Jordan*

Note:
*Staff members: Miss Spence, unidentified; and Mr. John Gavall, guitar. The
original document is in Special Collections, University of Cambridge Library.*

www.ingramcontent.com/pod-product-compliance
Lightning Source LLC
Chambersburg PA
CBHW060944090426

42738CB00024BA/3486

Nevada Bingo

Dayton	Silver	Las Vegas	Industry (-ies)	Henderson
Motto	Executive Branch	Sarah Winnemucca	Ichthyosaur	Indian Rice Grass
Lake Mead	Reno		State	Hoover Dam
Lake Tahoe	Mustang(s)	Tule Duck Decoy	Seal	Desert Bighorn
Quarter	Flag	Gemstone	Livestock	Kit Carson

Nevada Bingo

Great Basin National Park	Desert Tortoise	Comstock Lode	Flag	Sandstone
Pueblo Grande de Nevada	Dayton	Quarter	Virginia City	Executive Branch
Lake Mead	Desert Bighorn		Las Vegas	Border(s)
Kit Carson	Basin and Range	Sarah Winnemucca	Tule Duck Decoy	County (-ies)
State	Industry (-ies)	Seal	Silver	Boundary Peak

Nevada Bingo: Card No. 18

Nevada Bingo

Virginia City	Boundary Peak	Industry (-ies)	Hoover Dam	Tule Duck Decoy
Motto	Livestock	Pueblo Grande de Nevada	Gemstone	Ichthyosaur
Silver	Desert Tortoise		Battle Born State	Mark Twain
County (-ies)	State	Quarter	Reservation	Las Vegas
Border(s)	River(s)	Mustang(s)	Reno	Carson City

Nevada Bingo

Henderson	Silver	Livestock	Industry (-ies)	Carson City
Comstock Lode	Judicial Branch	Mountain Bluebird	Quarter	Sandstone
Kit Carson	Indian Rice Grass		Mining (-ed)	Basin and Range
Sierra Nevada	Virginia & Truckee Railroad	Song	Reservation	State
Trees	Reno	River(s)	Tule Duck Decoy	Las Vegas

Nevada Bingo: Card No. 20

Nevada Bingo

Motto	Boundary Peak	Mountain Bluebird	Industry (-ies)	Sierra Nevada
Kit Carson	Las Vegas	Columbia Plateau	Hoover Dam	Sagebrush
Desert Bighorn	Mustang(s)		Silver	Seal
Quarter	Gemstone	State	Lake Tahoe	Reno
Mining (-ed)	River(s)	Carson City	Dayton	Reservation

Nevada Bingo

Great Basin National Park	County (-ies)	Las Vegas	Border(s)	Flag
Sandstone	Livestock	Mark Twain	Hoover Dam	Battle Born State
Comstock Lode	Ichthyosaur		Sagebrush	Indian Rice Grass
State	Lake Tahoe	Reservation	Basin and Range	Mountain Bluebird
River(s)	Dayton	Silver	Desert Bighorn	Mining (-ed)

Nevada Bingo

Columbia Plateau	Silver	Gemstone	Border(s)	Carson City
Boundary Peak	Henderson	Mustang(s)	Motto	Basin and Range
County (-ies)	Flag		Song	Sagebrush
Desert Bighorn	River(s)	State	Dayton	Reservation
Sierra Nevada	Virginia & Truckee Railroad	Reno	Quarter	Las Vegas

Nevada Bingo

Columbia Plateau	Reno	Henderson	Silver	Hoover Dam
Las Vegas	Carson City	Mountain Bluebird	Sandstone	Sagebrush
Indian Rice Grass	Great Basin National Park		Flag	Desert Bighorn
Sierra Nevada	Song	State	Dayton	Kit Carson
Trees	Mining (-ed)	River(s)	Livestock	Virginia & Truckee Railroad

Nevada Bingo

Mining (-ed)	Mountain Bluebird	Silver	Seal	Las Vegas
Basin and Range	Kit Carson	Motto	Columbia Plateau	Battle Born State
Lake Tahoe	Hoover Dam		Song	State
Mark Twain	Sierra Nevada	Virginia & Truckee Railroad	River(s)	Ichthyosaur
Carson City	Henderson	Comstock Lode	Executive Branch	Trees

Nevada Bingo: Card No. 25

Nevada Bingo

Las Vegas	Silver	County (-ies)	Sandstone	Great Basin National Park
Quarter	Livestock	Hoover Dam	Henderson	Columbia Plateau
Lake Tahoe	Song		Ichthyosaur	Mining (-ed)
Dayton	Border(s)	Sierra Nevada	River(s)	State
Indian Rice Grass	Executive Branch	Seal	Virginia & Truckee Railroad	Trees

Nevada Bingo: Card No. 26

Nevada Bingo

County (-ies)	Comstock Lode	Silver	Henderson	Judicial Branch
Sierra Nevada	Song	Motto	State	Battle Born State
Sarah Winnemucca	Virginia & Truckee Railroad		River(s)	Mining (-ed)
Great Basin National Park	Boundary Peak	Mountain Bluebird	Trees	Basin and Range
Executive Branch	Ichthyosaur	Las Vegas	Mark Twain	Indian Rice Grass

Nevada Bingo

County (-ies)	Henderson	Mark Twain	Silver	Columbia Plateau
Judicial Branch	Las Vegas	Song	Sandstone	Ichthyosaur
Virginia & Truckee Railroad	Desert Bighorn		Indian Rice Grass	Quarter
Tule Duck Decoy	Great Basin National Park	Mustang(s)	River(s)	State
Border(s)	Lake Mead	Executive Branch	Trees	Sierra Nevada

Nevada Bingo: Card No. 28

Nevada Bingo

Las Vegas	Henderson	Great Basin National Park	Motto	Lake Mead
Reservation	Quarter	Mountain Bluebird	Indian Rice Grass	Mark Twain
Lake Tahoe	Song		Battle Born State	Silver
Judicial Branch	Sierra Nevada	Legislative Branch	River(s)	State
Columbia Plateau	Hoover Dam	Trees	Boundary Peak	Virginia & Truckee Railroad

Nevada Bingo

Desert Tortoise	Silver	Sandstone	Lake Mead	State
Basin and Range	Henderson	County (-ies)	Ichthyosaur	Battle Born State
Lake Tahoe	Flag		Indian Rice Grass	Mountain Bluebird
Trees	Boundary Peak	Border(s)	River(s)	Song
Sierra Nevada	Virginia City	Virginia & Truckee Railroad	Las Vegas	Mark Twain

Nevada Bingo: Card No. 30

www.ingramcontent.com/pod-product-compliance
Lightning Source LLC
LaVergne TN
LVHW061338060426
835511LV00014B/1991